Praise

St. Augustine rightly argu
a citizen of two cities or tv
the kingdom of man. In this ....
the kingdom of God works itself out in the life of the follower of
Christ so that he or she is able to live the kingdom out in the kingdom of man. This work presents a clearheaded, well-written theology of the kingdom of Christ that will compel our great King's
followers to live robust, joyful, gospel-driven lives to the glory of
God. Best of all, this work is deeply rooted in the text written by
the King of the kingdom—the Word of the living God. This book
will challenge, encourage, teach, convict you and spur its readers to
live in this age for the age to come.

JEFF ROBINSON
Senior Editor, The Gospel Coalition

Age of Crowns reveals our heart's longing to live for our true King
and His kingdom, yet without Jesus, we live as queens without a
king, a crown, a kingdom, or a castle. This book beautifully shows
how Jesus fulfills these God-designed longings in part now and in
fullness in eternity. Kori invites readers to embark on a glorious adventure with God and helps us live with more wonder and gratitude
for Jesus. This theologically rich and personally challenging book
will enlarge your vision of eternity and provide hope, purpose, and
courage in Jesus as we long for heaven.

HEATHER HOLLEMAN
Speaker, teacher, and author of *Seated with Christ: Living Freely in a
Culture of Comparison*

C. S. Lewis wisely said, "If you read history you will find that the
Christians who did most for the present world were precisely those
who thought most of the next." That's what Kori is accomplishing
in *Age of Crowns* . . . moving our focus from this world, filled with
the things of man, to the next world, which is filled with the treasures of God. Let this book strengthen you to take the next step
in your focus on the Age to Come. Live differently in your days on
earth as you center on the crowns of heaven instead of the chaos of
earth.

GREGG MATTE
Pastor of Houston's First Baptist Church
Author of *Unstoppable Gospel*

People I trust have continued to rave about Kori de Leon because she is a voice that young women should listen to—in fact, all of us should. She is educating and encouraging in her writing, and inspiring in her teaching. She knows what it is like to be loved and led by our King who gives dignity and purpose in all that He does. What I like best about Kori is that she is not out to leave a mark for herself, but rather for our God.

JONATHAN "JP" POKLUDA
Pastor at Watermark Community Church
Author of *Welcome to Adulting*

So many people today are attempting to find their identity and purpose in unhealthy places and in unhealthy ways. In *Age of Crowns*, Kori helps us understand that the desire to live for something bigger than ourselves has been placed within us by God and can only be discovered when we are rightly pursuing Jesus Christ and His kingdom. This book will take you on a journey of discovering of how living for the kingdom of God to come helps you make the most impact for the kingdom of God now.

JARRETT STEPHENS
Teaching Pastor, Prestonwood Baptist Church

Age of Crowns

PURSUING LIVES
MARKED BY
THE KINGDOM OF GOD

KORI DELEON

MOODY PUBLISHERS
CHICAGO

Unless otherwise noted, Scripture passages in this book are from The ESV® Bible (The Holy Bible, English Standard Version®). Copyright © 2001 by Crossway, a publishing ministry of Good News Publishers. Used by permission. All rights reserved.

Scripture quotations marked NASB are from the New American Standard Bible®. Copyright © 1960, 1962, 1963, 1968, 1971, 1972, 1973, 1975, 1977, 1995 by The Lockman Foundation. Used by permission. (www.Lockman.org)

Scripture quotations marked NIV are taken from the Holy Bible, New International Version®, NIV®. Copyright © 1973, 1978, 1984, 2011 by Biblica, Inc.™ Used by permission of Zondervan. All rights reserved worldwide. www.zondervan.com. The "NIV" and "New International Version" are trademarks registered in the United States Patent and Trademark Office by Biblica, Inc.™

Emphasis to Scripture has been added by the author.
Published in association with Don Gates at The Gates Group, www.gatesliterary.com.

Edited by Pamela J. Pugh
Interior design: Ragont Design
Cover design: Connie Gabbert Design and Illustration
Cover photo of starry sky by Stas Ovsky on Unsplash.

Library of Congress Cataloging-in-Publication Data

Names: De Leon, Kori, author.
Title: Age of crowns : pursuing lives marked by the kingdom of God / by Kori de Leon.
Description: Chicago : Moody Publishers, 2018. | Includes bibliographical references. |
Identifiers: LCCN 2017054980 (print) | LCCN 2018005259 (ebook) | ISBN 9780802496430 () | ISBN 9780802416858
Subjects: LCSH: Christian women--Religious life. | Adventure and adventurers--Miscellanea.
Classification: LCC BV4527 (ebook) | LCC BV4527 .D4 2018 (print) | DDC 248.8/43--dc23
LC record available at https://lccn.loc.gov/2017054980

ISBN: 978-0-8024-1685-8

We hope you enjoy this book from Moody Publishers. Our goal is to provide high-quality, thought-provoking books and products that connect truth to your real needs and challenges. For more information on other books and products written and produced from a biblical perspective, go to www.moodypublishers.com or write to:

Moody Publishers
820 N. LaSalle Boulevard
Chicago, IL 60610

1 3 5 7 9 10 8 6 4 2

Printed in the United States of America

In my early adulthood I had recurring dreams of our family walking with Christ during our youth. I never wanted to awake in the morning, because the what-could-have-been was so sweet to my soul. But when I came to awareness, a trail of grief would follow for the years that were lost due to sin. These dreams continued until the day I stopped looking backward and began looking forward. There are no words to communicate my gratitude to God for our family's salvation. I am in awe of the transformation He has worked and continues to work in your lives. And my heart melts with adoration for Jesus when I consider the what-will-be for us together with Dad in the Age to Come.

CONTENTS

1

PART 1

MADE FOR A GRAND ADVENTURE

CHAPTER 1

LONGING FOR THE AGE TO COME

We have all read . . . the story of the man who has forgotten his name. This man walks about the streets and can see and appreciate everything; only he cannot remember who he is. Well, every man is that man in the story. . . . We are all under the same mental calamity. . . .We have all forgotten what we really are.

—G. K. Chesterton

As G. K. Chesterton notes above, we're all familiar with stories in which someone has forgotten who he or she is—whether it's a fairy tale about being stolen from the royal family as a child or a contemporary story of someone suffering from dementia in adulthood.

In many of these stories, the woman has moments when she vaguely remembers her heritage or original state, but then quickly slips back into the darkness of her mental calamity. And often in these stories, there is someone who loves the woman with an unfailing love—someone who is longing for her and working to bring her back to her true reality.

To paraphrase G. K. Chesterton, we are all like the woman in these stories.[1] Due to sin, we have suffered a mental calamity, like spiritual amnesia, if you will. We have forgotten who we really are. We have forgotten God and His glorious design for us. But there are moments when our hearts are stirred with deep desires to return to someone great . . . something glorious for which we seem to be made, but we cannot find our way home because our hearts and minds have become darkened toward God due to our sin against Him (Rom. 1:21; Eph. 4:18). Something has gone wrong with the human race—something is not right within us or in the world.

But we are not without hope. God breathes clarity and understanding through the truth in His Word. And what we learn in the Bible is that humanity does indeed have glorious origins. And there is Someone who loves us and is working to bring us back to our true reality; namely, Jesus Christ.

In view of this good news, let's consider four desires that are common to humanity, desires that point to our glorious origins; desires that cause us to long and yearn for the far greater life God designed for us to share with Him.

A QUEEN WITHOUT A KING

Many women desire a relationship with a kinglike man. We want to be united with someone who is stunning; someone who will love us, lead us, and protect us as we take grand adventures with him. This is a natural longing, built in because God is the King of the world and He made us to live in a glorious relationship with Him.[2] But humanity threw off God's lordship and love, exchanging God the Creator for the lesser, created things. So we set off to find someone or something in creation to make us happy and help us flourish rather than God.

When we begin to recognize that our experiences in this world do not align with our grand desires, we become disillusioned.

And if we do not grasp the reason for our grand longings to be in a relationship with a glorious King and why our lives fall short (which is because of sin—our own and that in the world), we will respond in a destructive way. We'll begin to recalibrate our standards. In other words, we will lower our criteria and set off on a new journey—not to find the perfect One, but just to find one who will do.

Though we try to silence the yearning in our hearts to find the perfect One, our desires will not have it. They will continue to protest with loud cries of dissatisfaction and discontentment, pleading with us to remember that we are in fact made for a great King. Perhaps you have heard people articulate the tension between our grand longings and fallen lives with the common phrase, "I feel like a queen without a king." Can you relate?

When God created humanity, He made us in His image so we could know Him and relate with Him.

A QUEEN WITHOUT A CROWN

God bestowed great dignity and worth on us by creating us in His image. And we see remnants of this truth in our common human desire for a sense of dignity. People want to be valued and perceived by others as having worth and honor. Yet we may find ourselves struggling with feeling unimportant, undervalued, disrespected, and living in undignified ways. So let's take a closer look at where dignity comes from and why it seems that we have fallen from it.

When God created humanity, He made us in His image so we could know Him and relate with Him. But He also made us in His image to be like Him. Does this take your breath away? If it doesn't, perhaps you do not yet have eyes to see the glory of God that has been stamped on you—and on every man, woman, and child.

All throughout Scripture, God makes a distinction between humanity and the rest of creation by setting us apart as having special worth—not in and of ourselves, but because we bear His image. There can be no higher form of dignity than being made in the likeness of the Dignified One! Let me say that another way: God is the most excellent and glorious Being. And we are made to image-forth His likeness throughout the world.

John Calvin said it was already a great thing that God gave man the highest place among creatures, but "it is a nobility far more exalted, that he should bear resemblance to his Creator, as a son does to his father."[3] Calvin concludes it is not possible for God to act more generously to man than by impressing His own glory upon us.

The Bible sometimes uses "crown" to symbolize the honor and dignity God bestowed on human beings by making us in His image and giving us the high privilege of reflecting His character and rule throughout the world. For example, in Old Testament times, high priests in Israel as well as kings wore crowns.

But when God's people live in ways that are contrary to the dignified King, the Bible describes our loss of dignity and honor this way: "The crown has fallen from our head; woe to us, for we have sinned!" (Lam. 5:16).

A QUEEN WITHOUT A KINGDOM

We also have longings to be part of something great and to accomplish grand works, to cultivate, develop, and rule over something significant. We want to develop our children, cultivate our home, build a business, lead inspiring movements, and much more. Yet why do our lives often seem mundane and meaningless?

When God created us in His image, He also gave us the mandate to subdue the earth and rule over it as His representatives in subjection to Him (Gen. 1:26–28). But humanity became prideful. When we threw off God's rule over our lives, we lost the right to rule in subjection to Him. In other words, we lost dominion. Now we are like deposed kings and queens in a fallen world, who pridefully seek to build our own kingdoms, for our own glory, and for our own fleeting fame.

A QUEEN WITHOUT A CASTLE

A fourth longing common to women—and to humanity in general—is our desire to live in a beautiful and safe place and to have access to abundant material resources, perhaps remembering our original home, the garden of Eden. But the garden of Eden was more than just a place of beauty and bounty; it was the place where the King lived in a rich relationship with His people. Its abundance was not only due to its resources and beauty, but because it was the place where humanity lived in the presence of God. But when humanity was unfaithful to Him, we were exiled from our glorious home with Him.

Creation was subjected to futility, and humanity has experienced a poverty of place[4] ever since. In many ways, we have experienced a poverty of material resources as well. In a sense, our souls seem to know that we have more glorious origins. But friction is apparent between our longings and our fallen lives, causing us to groan for a better world and a sense of true home.

UNBLUSHING PROMISES

The Bible reveals that there are ancient roots and future cords connected to these longings that continue to tug and pull on our hearts. In other words, the reason we long for a King, crown, kingdom, and castle is because we were made for God and His kingdom. When humanity became arrogant and attempted to have these things apart from God, our desires became soiled by sin. But that's not the end of the story—indeed, it is only the beginning!

Jesus, the only Son of God, died to pay the penalty for sin. Those who repent of their sin and put their trust in Jesus for their salvation will be forgiven and reconciled back to God. Jesus came to lead us back to the indescribable pleasures of knowing Him so our hearts will echo David who said, "The LORD is my chosen portion and my cup; you hold my lot. The lines have fallen for me in pleasant places; indeed, I have a beautiful inheritance" (Ps. 16:5–6). And we are called to the adventure of new life with Him: "You make known to me the path of life; in your [God's] presence there is fullness of joy; at your right hand are pleasures forevermore" (v. 11).

The gift of salvation and its many blessings begin today in the lives of those who believe. God begins re-creating us in His image and redeeming our lives to reflect His good design for us. And while we do dream of building families, dwelling places, and careers/ministries for the exaltation of His name, we must remember that we are living in a fallen world that is perishing (1 Cor. 7:29–31). In other words, we need to dream and build in view of the Age to Come. Jesus contrasts "this age" with "the age to come" in glorious ways. And to use C. S. Lewis's words, Jesus makes "unblushing promises of reward" that will be enjoyed by His people in the Age to Come.

GAZING BEYOND THE STARS

The Age to Come is described as a gift for God's people. It will be an age when believers in Jesus Christ will enter into the full measure of blessing that comes from living under God's good rule, which will be manifested throughout the new world.[5] In Matthew 12:32 Jesus refers to two ages when He says "either in *this age,* or in *the age to come.*" In Luke 20:35–38 Jesus says that those who "are considered worthy to attain to that age" will become immortal. Let me slow down and say that again: we will never experience death again!

And Jesus promised that those who have left everything to follow Him and advance the gospel will receive a hundredfold "now in this time," and "in the age to come eternal life" (Mark 10:30). As we can see, Jesus makes a clear distinction between this age and the Age to Come. And we are called to set our minds on the things that are above and to live in view of them (Col. 3:2).

Therefore, I want to invite you to dream beyond the stars with me! Let's enter into the vivid pictures in the Bible of far greater things to come. Let's consider the age of crowns by mentally gazing upon the King. Let's marvel at the royal family God is creating who will rule with Him forever. Let's walk through the majestic city of

God, which will become the famous metropolis of the world.

Then we will come back down to earth by considering inspiring ways to live and prepare for our coming King and His kingdom now. Our purpose here is not to focus on when these events will happen or how they will unfold—let's savor the fact that they will!

KINGS, QUEENS, CROWNS, CASTLES?

I love how C. S. Lewis describes Jesus as "unblushing" in His promises of reward. When a person is embarrassed, he or she may blush. And isn't this true of how we may feel when we begin to believe and share Christ's claims concerning the King, crown, kingdom, and castles to come? God's promises and rewards are so grand that they can make us blush to repeat them for fear of being perceived as living in a fairy tale ourselves.

In my pre-Christ days I would have rolled my eyes and smirked with distaste toward an adult nonfiction book that discussed kings, queens, crowns, and castles. I had always had a strong taste for reality and living authentically with it.

But the only reality I knew was our fragmented, fallen reality, and authenticity meant acknowledging—at some level—that we are a broken mess. Therefore, to talk about the stuff of royalty in application to broken people would have been embarrassing and seemingly delusional—like insecure women trying to be something they are not.

After graduating from college, I moved to Houston, Texas, to begin my postgraduate career. By this time, I had tasted enough disappointments from creation's inability to fulfill my desires that I had begun recalibrating my standards at frighteningly low levels and settling further into the sinful slums of the world. But then one night a coworker invited me to a Bible study. Through a series of events that took place over a four-month period, I heard and believed the gospel for the first time. And something powerful took place in my life. I was awakened to reality, much as the apostle Paul describes:

"Awake, O sleeper,
and arise from the dead,
and Christ will shine on you."
(Ephesians 5:14)

Looking back, I can see irony all over that moment. For being such a lover of reality, I had been living in La La Land. Due to sin, my mind was darkened toward God. I knew God existed, but that reality seemed dull to me. Thus, I lived as though I was the center of my own universe. I also knew I was sinful and broken. But I had created a false reality by thinking there would be no penalty for my sin. I flattered myself by believing that I would be received into heaven because I had never done anything heinous like taken the life of another—even though I had broken all God's other good laws! And though I would have agreed that God is the ruler of the universe, I determined for myself what was right and wrong and how I would live each day.

But when I heard the gospel, I was awakened to reality, where God is gloriously alive and active and the world is bright

When a person is reconciled to God through Jesus Christ, she will begin to experience such depths of love in her relationship with Him that she does not need anything else to satisfy her.

with beauty, adventure, and a good future for those who live in submission to Him. Jesus graciously brought me out of the fragmented truths and false realities I had created for myself. At the time, I did not have a biblical vocabulary to articulate what was happening. I could only describe what I was experiencing.

I remember fumbling to find words to describe the experience to my unbelieving friends. "I feel like I am alive for the first time in my life. When I was at the Bible study listening to the message, it was as if someone took a defibrillator and jolted me to life—everything looks brighter, the world seems beautiful . . . I don't know how to explain it, and I know it sounds strange . . . but I don't feel hate in my heart anymore . . . and I want to start knowing God."

It wasn't long before my life began to give evidence to the fact that something truly did change within me. When my friends and I went to clubs, I didn't want to partake in all the same things I did before, but I was happy to dance sober by their side. And it did not take long before the dark and dingy atmosphere of our gatherings became distasteful compared to my new life with God, who was beckoning me to bright adventures with Him. Looking back, I can see that my life was bearing witness to the truth of Scripture. The Bible perfectly explains what happened to me when I heard and believed the gospel (see Eph. 2:1–5).

A SOCIETY OF PRAISE

When a person is reconciled to God through Jesus Christ, she will begin to experience such depths of love in her relationship with Him that she does not need anything else to satisfy her—the thought of kingdoms, crowns, and castles fade away due to the pleasures she experiences in the presence of her King.

These moments are foretastes of what life will be like *all the time* when we live face to face with Jesus. But when we spend time with our King through His Word, He begins to tell us astonishing news. He tells us about secondary rewards that He will lavish on those who love, seek, and obey Him—which begin now and will be consummated in the Age to Come.

For example, God promises to reward those who seek Him with citizenship in His majestic city, membership in His royal family, significant roles in His kingdom, and more. So how does this all work together? Is Jesus reward enough, or does He bless us even further and give us rewards in creation?

Without faith it is impossible to please him, for whoever would draw near to God must believe that he exists and that he rewards those who seek him. (Hebrews 11:6)

God created the physical world to reveal Himself to us (Rom. 1:20). C. S. Lewis helps us understand how creation leads us to worship God by describing the things in creation as "signposts" that point us to God.[6] In other words, when we look at the vast universe and splendorous stars, we know the God who made them is powerful and divine. The universe is filled with glorious features that tell us who God is and what He is like so we can enjoy Him more fully.

However, fallen humanity uses creation wrongly. We seek created things to be our substitutes for God, which is idolatry (Rom. 1:23). But God is forgiving people's sin through Jesus Christ and re-creating us to relate with creation properly. In the Age to Come, we will live in a new world with glorious rewards such as cities, crowns, palaces, and more. And all these staggering rewards in creation will not lead us to forget God; rather, they will lead us to know and enjoy Him more fully![7]

With all this in mind, I would like to invite you to join me on a journey of walking through the stunning features of life in the Age to Come.

And get ready to worship, because if we consider these things properly, they will lead us to become a society of praise for our King, resulting in the fame of His name, and awaken us to live more fully for His kingdom now!

"FAIRY-TALE PHILOSOPHER"

Using Chesterton's language, I would like to invite you to join me in becoming a "fairy-tale philosopher."[8] I love this paradoxical phrase! At first glance it sounds like two opposite concepts. People often think of *fairy tales* as naïve. Yet, *philosophers* are perceived as being intellectually sophisticated because they are people who think deeply about life.

I think this phrase is fitting for Christians. God has given us the answers to the most important questions in life through His Word. Thus, we are people who think deeply about life. And what we find in Scripture and therefore believe to be true is that living under the lordship of a glorious King as His queen with crowns and castles restored by His grace is in fact the destiny of believers. And while this may sound naïve to the world—like the stuff of fairy tales—it is in fact a profound reality to which our deepest longings and pursuits testify to each day.

I am not suggesting that we become women who are led by emotional longings or fanciful stories. Rather, I am echoing Chesterton by noting that there are some parts of fairy tales that mimic the world of wonder God has designed. And while fairy tales fail to tell the complete story, the Bible brings the universal story together in a comprehensive and glorious way.

As fairy-tale philosophers, let's approach the Word of God as a book full of wonder because a God

Let's approach the Word of God as a book full of wonder because a God of wonder authored it.

of wonder authored it. Let's read the Bible with utmost care, not twisting it and turning it to say what we want it to say. No, no, no, the wonders of God and His design for the world are far greater than anything we can imagine on our own. Let's seek God through His Word, ready to read epic stories because they are part of God's grand adventure. And let's seek to become well-versed in kings and queens, castles and crowns, the moral lessons of the sacrifices we make in this fallen world for our true Love, and how to live for Christ's kingdom—which has already begun in our midst, giving us foretastes of the fullness to come.

DRAWING UP DESIRES

We long for the stuff of kings, crowns, kingdoms, and castles because we were made for God and His kingdom. But due to sin, we seek to have these things apart from Him. Let's identify our idols and begin exchanging that time and energy for pursuing God and His kingdom (1 Tim. 4:8). And in doing so, we will discover great reward (Heb. 11:6).

1. We discussed four desires that are common to humanity. Which one(s) are you longing for and seeking to obtain during your current season of life (a king, crown, kingdom, or castle)?

2. Are you lowering your standards and searching for someone or something other than God and His kingdom to satisfy the high desires of your heart? If yes, what things in creation are you turning to for satisfaction? In other words, how are you settling for less?

3. James 4:1–3 says we are inwardly frustrated and fight with others when we do not get what we selfishly desire. Do you find yourself frustrated in your endeavors or relationships? Which ones? The heart of frustration is often due to unmet expectations, which can be rooted in pride and idolatry.

4. Another way to identify our idols is to consider the things we turn to when the pressures of life begin to squeeze us. Take time to recount three recent circumstances when you felt life's pressures. Who or what did you turn to for relief?

5. Let's consider one more avenue for identifying idols of our heart. Which of the desires described above are you so eager to satisfy that you are willing to sin for it?

Hebrews 11:6 tells us that God wants us to draw near to Him with confidence, knowing He exists and is a Rewarder of those who seek Him. I would like to invite you to confess your sin to God, marvel at His rewarding nature, and prepare your heart to seek Him and His kingdom with more devotion in the days to come!

CHAPTER 2

POWERFUL PICTURES OF THE AGE TO COME

If then you have been raised with Christ, seek the things that are above, where Christ is, seated at the right hand of God. Set your minds on things that are above, not on things that are on earth.

—Colossians 3:12

I recently went to a high school graduation. The stadium was filled with young men and women ready to launch their ships into the sea of life. It was fascinating to hear the language of the four desires described in chapter 1 woven throughout many of the students' speeches.

They talked about fulfilling great purpose, venturing into beautiful parts of the world, and seeking a significant relationship along the way. But none of them mentioned God. They each pointed to self as the determiner of their course, the source of strength for the journey, and the recipient of honor for any progress made.

Sails were being set with energy and excitement to search for kings, crowns, kingdoms, and castles—apart from God. I could not help but see myself years ago standing alongside of them. I was ready to search for the good life but did not know which course would lead me there. To be honest, if someone had given me a Bible and said something as pointed as this: "Read this book from God. He will guide you and empower you to take the one adventure that leads to the destiny you long for," I think I would have pridefully set it aside, eager to go my own way.

The current of sin ran powerfully through my veins. And so I set off to search for someone or something in this world to make me happy and help me flourish, only to find myself chasing after the wind.

One such adventure took place in my young twenties. The course was set when my friends and I went to Panama City Beach, Florida, for spring break our junior year in college. When I stepped onto the sugar-white sand, looked upon the emerald-green waters, and breathed the sea air into my lungs, I felt seized and set free at the same time. Beauty and adventure were alive all around us in the crashing waves, colorful skies, singing birds, and the sounds of boats. My heart was hooked in a mere moment and a desire was awakened to find a king—a handsome man—to enjoy these idyllic surroundings with me.

My friends and I returned the next two summers. We lived across the street from the emerald waters and were employed as lifeguards on the beach so we could play at work and work at play. It was not long before we became identified as semilocals, since we were there for the full summer, while the majority of other vacationers were in and out within a week.

Our new group of friends were people who worked the restaurants and clubs and who managed rentals on the beach, such as jet skis and boats. Thus our friendships developed into a laissez-faire system of bartering and trading, which enabled us all the more to go where we wanted to go and do what we wanted to do. There was a time when we seemed to be kings and queens of our own worlds—free, independent, and charged with unending energy in a place that was alive with beauty and adventure.

It was not long before the beauty of the beach became routine. Like all things in creation, it did not ultimately satisfy us.

But it was not long before the beauty of the beach became routine. Like all things in creation, it did not ultimately satisfy us. And so we began playing less by day and seeking more adventure by night—sliding further into our sensuality and being driven by our passions. Before we knew it, the harsh lovers of drink, fallen relationships, and the consequences that followed became a taskmaster over us.

Toward the end of summer, most seasonal workers returned home for the new school year, though a few of us remained for a couple of extra weeks. One evening when my friends and I walked into a bar, what I noticed powerfully impacted me. The place was filled with some true locals—people who lived on the beach year round—ranging from about forty to seventy years old. Their skin was leathery from years in the sun, and they were *still* driven by sensuality, reveling in drunkenness, looking for someone to accompany them home at night. Though the deceptive beauty of seeking a king and castle on the coast apart from God had begun to sink its bitter fangs into my soul earlier in the summer, this was the moment that my delusion was fully exposed.

Looking back, I can see the gracious King in pursuit of me even when I was walking deep in my sin and separated from Him.

He allowed my sinful pursuits to become bitter and gave me a preview of where such a life would lead; namely, emptiness and ruin. By doing so, God turned my heart away from returning for a third summer to seek my happiness with broken kings in a fleeting, paradisiacal palace, though I still had one more godless journey in me. But what I found at the end of all my godless pursuits was always the same: apart from God, nothing ends well, nothing ends happy, and nothing ends right.

LOOKING UP

Perhaps this part of my story has called forth memories of godless journeys of your own. Young men and women are full of energy and set off on many adventures to search for the good life. But we have two powerful things working against us: (1) our sin nature that runs through our veins, seeking happiness in kings, crowns, kingdoms, and castles apart from God, and (2) demonic forces enticing our desires through deceptive forms of beauty to seek these things apart from God, ultimately leading to our death and destruction (see James 1:14–15; 2 Cor. 11:3).

But God has given believers the gifts of the indwelling of the Holy Spirit, a new heart that is inclined to love God, and staggering images of the Age to Come to serve as a powerful arsenal to help women avoid the deceitful journeys that take us far from home and motivate us to take the one journey that leads to the destiny we long for.[1]

> If then you have been raised with Christ, *seek the things* that are above, where Christ is, seated at the right hand of God.

Set your minds on things that are above, not on things that are on earth. (Col. 3:1–2)

God tells us to focus our minds on Christ and His staggering promises of the glories to come. Doing so will help us begin to understand *why* we have desires for the stuff of kings, crowns, kingdoms, and castles—it is in fact the origin of humanity and the destiny of believers!

God's Word also convicts us of pursuing these things apart from Him. The Holy Spirit will begin to anchor our hearts to Jesus and the glories to come. And as Colossians 3:1 reveals, this will not result in some sort of dreamy state of inactivity and uselessness. No, we will be moved to *seek* God's presence and kingdom now.

WHEN THE LIGHT SHIFTS

Do you remember the joy of a new day when you were a child? I do! The morning light shining through the blinds would awaken me and call me to the adventures of an exciting new day. I would spring out of bed, pull on my clothes, and ride my bike to meet my friends. We would take whatever adventure came to us that day—exploring canyons, playing in tree houses, jumping off ropes into sandpit ponds. The day was bright and full of opportunities.

But inevitably a moment came when the sun would subtly shift to dim shades of orange and yellow like a celestial clock, reminding us that our time was coming to an end. The crisp and invigorating morning air had given way to the tired afternoon heat. And all of a sudden we would realize we had played the day away. With a sense of disappointment, we packed up our belongings and returned to our homes to settle in for the night.

In a similar way, when we are young, our perspective is often bright and full of opportunities because there seems to be ample time to go where we want and do what we want, and because our bodies are full of energy, we are ready to go where the wind of adventure blows. But one day—usually around midlife—we realize we have played a good portion of our life away. If our minds are set on "things that are on earth," then we certainly will become anxious, discouraged, or depressed.

LOOKING IN

Setting our minds on these "things that are above" will have rich rewards for young women—in their present and future life.

But doing so also has powerful benefits for those in midlife and beyond. We may take many journeys during our youth. But then around our middle years, we begin to take stock. We even begin to consider our mortality. All of a sudden we notice that our bodies are beginning to change. Our options in life begin to narrow. We may have selected our spouse and, in many cases, have had all the children we are going to have. Perhaps we have advanced as far as we are going to go in our careers.

And we may even have to acknowledge that some of the dreams we once envisioned may never come true. Can you relate to any of this?

This realization can creep up on us quickly. Trying to articulate what is happening is tough, let alone understanding how to overcome its perplexities. Weird things just begin to happen, like receiving an email from an ex-boyfriend you haven't talked to since high school, people—even professing Christians—talking about divorce, friends who begin withdrawing from relationships as if letting down their sail of adventure and packing it away for an early night. And others try to soothe the frightening feeling that life is slipping through their fingers with a last few big gulps of the world. What is happening here?

We are looking at today only.

LOOKING AHEAD

Consider how different life looks when we set our eyes on tomorrow—the eternal day! God has filled the Scriptures with bright pictures of tomorrow. He has given us thrilling previews of the day when believers will stand face to face with Jesus our King. He has provided us with rich preludes of the city of God and calls us to "walk about Zion and go around her . . . go through her palaces" (Ps. 48:12–13 NASB). God has given us bright pictures of the eternal day and calls us to set our eyes on them.

> All glorious is the princess in her chamber, with robes interwoven with gold. In many-colored robes she is led to the king. . . . With joy and gladness they are led along as they enter the palace of the king. (Psalm 45:13–15)

So how do we go about setting our minds on the things that are above? Let's answer this question by discussing the power of pictures and then conclude by considering how to set our minds on the powerful pictures that God has given to us in the Bible.

POWERFUL PICTURES FROM A PERFECT BOOK

My six-year-old daughter Jade listens to audio books to give her a pleasant escape from rush-hour traffic in Houston. I often smile when I glance in the rearview mirror and see her sitting in the back seat; she is there, but not there. Her mind is in a faraway land. Her inner person has entered the kingdom of Camelot and is enjoying adventures with unicorns, dragons, and knights. I love watching her, amazed at her God-given ability to imagine another world and to do so in a way that she is, in a sense, taken to Camelot and experiencing the adventure herself . . . until someone honks their horn, bringing her back to the drudgery of Houston traffic.

God has given our minds the stunning ability to see or envision. Yes, we can see the present. But we can also picture the past as well as things yet to come. When someone tells us about a past event, we can visualize it. When someone describes their plans for the future, we can go there with them in our minds.

Now, logical statements are certainly important for gaining a rational understanding of God and the world He has designed. But our understanding is greatly enhanced when these truths are communicated and illustrated through stories and pictures. Images have a powerful way of bringing us into them where we can taste, see, and experience the truth for ourselves. You could read a definition of love, which is important to help you understand the concept. But when we read a story or see images in a movie of a man and a woman in love with each other, we are somehow brought into the story to taste and experience love for ourself.

So we see that pictures and images are powerful in general. But consider with me the surpassing power of biblical pictures! The Bible is not simply another book written by man; it is written by God.[2] He has given us visionary literature so we can imagine things that have not yet happened. As Leland Ryken notes, visionary literature calls us to use our imaginations to "fly beyond the stars" by picturing a transformed world, a change of fortunes that is beyond our present reality. It "shakes us out of complacency."[3]

Combine the power of pictures and images of the Age to Come with the power of God's Word. The result? We are drawn into these future realities to taste and experience them for ourselves while the Holy Spirit shakes us out of complacency and works powerful results in our hearts—some of which are described in Psalm 19 as reviving our soul, making the simple wise, rejoicing the heart, enlightening our eyes, warning us so we can escape judgment and loss, and teaching us how to live so as to receive great reward (vv. 7, 8, 11). How does the Holy Spirit use the pictures of the Age to Come to revive, rejoice, and enlighten our hearts (vv. 7–8)? Consider Paul's stunning statement in 1 Corinthians 2:9–10:

"What no eye has seen, nor ear heard, nor the heart of man imagined, what God has prepared for those who love him"— these things God has revealed to us through the Spirit.

God is preparing glorious things for His people in the Age to Come—far greater than anything we could dream for ourselves—a life full of wondrous things like kings and queens, castles and crowns. These glorious things are revealed to us by the illuminating work of the Holy Spirit through God's Word in the Bible. When the Spirit enlightens our eyes to the day when we will be face to face with Jesus Christ—the most excellent of men—and when the Spirit walks us through the city of God— the glorious metropolis of the coming world—our hearts will be given over to revival and ecstatic joy!

The Holy Spirit will also use the pictures of the Age to Come to warn us so we can escape judgment and loss, while teaching us how to live in such a way that we will receive great reward (Ps. 19:11). In chapter 10, we will enter into some of the stories and pictures Jesus shares concerning the judgment of believers. All believers will stand before God to be assessed for how we lived in this life.

Because we are saved by grace not by works (Eph. 2:8–9), Christ's assessment of a believer's life will not pertain to salvation. But God will reward and recompense each believer for what we did while in the body, good or evil (2 Cor. 5:9–11). And as far-reaching as this sounds, Jesus tells us that these rewards will determine things, such as how many cities we rule over in the Age to Come (Luke 19:16–17). When the Holy Spirit leads us into the biblical teaching of the judgment seat of Christ and pictures that describe the coming assessment, He

will create humility and a healthy fear of the
Lord in our hearts. We will be motivated to
turn away from evil and make it our aim to
please God (Ezek. 11:19; 36:26; Jer. 31:33;
Heb. 8:10).

Pictures of the Age to Come are powerful because they are
God-breathed and will not leave us unchanged! For this reason,
I am eager for us to set our minds on the things to come. And I
echo the prayer of the apostle Paul, asking God to enlighten the
eyes of our hearts so we may know the hope to which He has
called us, the riches of the glorious inheritance of God's people
(Eph. 1:18–19). So let's talk for a moment about how to set our
minds on the staggering features of life in the Age to Come.

PONDER, PICTURE, AND PRAY

Psalm 1 introduces the psalms as a whole and begins with an
important instruction for experiencing the good life. We are to
meditate on God's Word. The happy person is the one whose
"delight is in the law of the LORD, and on his law he *meditates* day
and night" (v. 2).

Eastern meditation is an emptying of the mind. But one significant problem with this form of meditation is that our fallen
minds are full of evil thoughts! Therefore, we need to do much
more than just empty our minds. We need to renew our minds
with God's Word so we can discern that which is true, good, and
beautiful (Rom. 12:2; Phil. 4:8).

Jerry and Marilyn Fine explain that biblical meditation means to ponder, picture, and pray.[4] We are to think on what God is telling us, form a mental *picture* of God's Word in our mind, and *pray*, or talk to God about it. Then the rest of the psalms roll out with rich and powerful pictures—some that are prophetic pictures of the Age to Come—for us to enter into so we can mentally gaze on, taste, and be shaped by reality, where God is alive and the world is full of wonder and thrilling hope with Him.

Thus, Scripture teaches that the happy person is the one who has a fervent relationship with God through His Word. As we sow God's Word into our minds, we will reap a harvest of joyful kingdom living both now and later in the Age to Come.

But meditating on God's Word takes discipline. Until believers are perfected in heaven, we have two kinds of appetites (Gal. 5:16–25). We have a sinful appetite to seek and find our king, kingdom, crown, and castle apart from God in the things of this world. But believers also have a new appetite. Our new self in Christ longs to live under His good lordship. Therefore, God teaches us to put off the old self and put on the new (Eph. 4:23–24). But until we step into the fullness of our salvation, we have to fight our sin nature and *discipline* ourselves to stay awake to reality (1 Tim. 4:7–8).

> **Begin meditating on the glorious life to come; stay awake to reality, because God is real.**

Remaining awake to reality is an important truth the apostle Paul talks about in Ephesians 5:14–17.

"Awake, O sleeper, and arise from the dead, and Christ will shine on you." Look carefully then how you walk, not as unwise but as wise, making the best use of the time, because the days are evil. Therefore do not be foolish, but understand what the will of the Lord is.

Based on this verse, C. S. Lewis talks about coming awake to reality with God and remaining awake.[5] Kevin Vanhoozer says that, for Lewis, "waking is a way of describing one's conversion, a coming to new life. The Christian life is all about wakefulness." Once we are awake, we begin to study theology, which "describes what we see when we are awake." In this way, "discipleship is the project of becoming *fully* awake to this reality and *staying* awake."[6]

Thus, I invite you to begin meditating with me on the glorious life to come; to stay awake to reality, because God is real, and He is calling us to kingdom adventures with Him now.

But staying awake to reality requires discipline, which can be challenging at first, like many things in life that are good for us.

POWERFUL MEDITATION

I am one of those strange people who actually likes vegetables. But what is interesting is that I was raised in the Midwest—we ate meat and potatoes growing up! Eating more vegetables would require time and energy to learn how to prepare and cook them in an appetizing way. In other words, it would have required *discipline* to develop this new habit in my adulthood. As a result, I put it off for many years.

But one day I had a wake-up call. My dermatologist found precancerous cells on my lip due to years of enjoying the sun without protecting my skin. By God's grace, the condition was treatable, but the experience motivated me to become disciplined to healthier eating. As a result, I dove into the world of veggies and love it—my hunger is satiated most of the day, and I have much more energy.

In a similar way, when I became a Christian, I took a class on spiritual disciplines. We were taught some different ways to relate with God and experience Him in this life. We learned how to read, study, meditate on, and memorize God's Word, as well as the disciplines of prayer and fasting. My favorite was meditating. I was amazed by how powerful it was to picture God's Word, ponder it, and pray it back to Him. However, once the class ended, I rarely engaged in this activity, which I had enjoyed so much.

Reading and talking were not new concepts to me. So it was easier to spend the majority of my devotional time reading God's Word and talking to Him through prayer. But meditation seemed somewhat foreign to me and therefore required more *discipline* to develop the new habit. Therefore, in my laziness, I failed to do it. However, what I have since then realized is that though we might not name the practice, we actually engage in envisioning and meditating all the time!

We often escape in our minds imagining, tasting, and experiencing a wide variety of fantasies. A woman can dream about a life of being married to a different man. People can even spend time tasting and touching others in their mind through pornographic images.

We can sit for hours mentally creating new homes or renovating old ones, leading to frustration when we come back to our real home and face the fact that finances are too tight to make these dreams a reality. We can sit on the couch and watch movies for hours to find a place for us to live vicariously through the adventure and romance of others.

We can devote a great deal of our days imagining the possibility of accomplishing grand dreams and the fame that follows, often resulting in nurturing dissatisfaction toward our actual lives.

As you can see, we already envision and meditate all the time. But we will create and perpetuate a great deal of sin, loneliness, dissatisfaction, and frustration in our hearts by envisioning, imagining, or meditating on unbiblical thoughts and fantasies instead of meditation on the glories of what is and what is to come.[7] And the more we soak our minds in misdirected meditations, the more our mind moves us to pursue these things because we want to experience them in reality.

When God calls us to meditate, He teaches us to do so in a good and powerful way—the way that leads us to glorify God and results in bright perspectives, pure pleasures, spiritual energy, courageous living, eternal rewards, and eagerness for the eternal day to come. What a staggering invitation! God calls us to come out of our disappointing and delusional lives and to step into the glorious reality He has designed.

Can you imagine what your life will begin to look like when you start taking steps to begin saturating your mind with the bright reality of Jesus Christ our good King?

Can you imagine what your life will begin to look like when you start taking steps to begin saturating your mind with

the bright reality of Jesus Christ our good King
who God says you are now
who He says you will be

His great kingdom works taking place in our midst
and the glories to come?

It will take discipline. But God tells us there are rich rewards
in the present life, as well as the life to come, for those who discipline themselves for godliness.

> Train yourself for godliness; for while bodily training is of
> some value, godliness is of value in every way, as it holds
> promise for the present life and also for the life to come.
> (1 Tim. 4:7–8)

A POWERFUL PRAYER

In 2 Samuel 7 God reveals to David His magnificent plan to create
a house or dynasty through David, which is a pinnacle promise
of God on which this book is built. Please take a few moments to
read that powerful chapter now.

God's promises concerning the glorious destiny of His
people that include a King, crown, and kingdom, flow from
the promise God made to David in this passage. And David's
response is beautiful:

> "Because of your promise, and according to your own heart,
> you have brought about all this greatness, to make your ser-
> vant know it. Therefore you are great, O LORD God. For
> there is none like you, and there is no God besides you,
> according to all that we have heard with our ears." (2 Sam.
> 7:21–22)

Who is like our God?! There is no one like our God, who is great and delights to do good to His people (Isa. 64:4). Let's continue:

> "For you, O LORD of hosts, the God of Israel, have made this revelation to your servant, saying, 'I will build you a house.' Therefore your servant has found courage to pray this prayer to you. And now, O Lord GOD, you are God, and your words are true, and you have promised this good thing to your servant. Now therefore may it please you to bless the house of your servant, so that it may continue forever before you. For you, O Lord GOD, have spoken, and with your blessing shall the house of your servant be blessed forever." (2 Sam. 7:27–29)

I love David's humble and courageous prayer to God. How can it be that you have promised such grand things to me? he marvels. Yet since you are God and your words are true, I have courage to pray your promise back to You.

David prays that God would be pleased to do the good and grand things He has promised to David and his dynasty.

I invite you to join me in imitating David's prayer. God has given us magnificent revelations of the destiny He has designed for believers in Jesus Christ. God calls us to set our minds upon His glorious promises and powerful pictures and live in view of them. Therefore, may we have courage to pray that God will enlighten our eyes to see our glorious inheritance and to enable us to live more devoted to Him today as we prepare for the age of crowns to come. Let's pray together:

Heavenly Father, You are wonderful. And Your design for our lives is so grand that it can take courage to even pray it back to You. We know our sinful origins and that we do not deserve the extravagant grace You are pleased to lavish on us through Jesus Christ. But we acknowledge with David that You are God and Your Word is true. And so we pray that You would open the eyes of our hearts to see the glorious destiny You have designed for believers and empower us to pursue lives marked by Your kingdom for Your glory. Amen!

MENTAL MUSING

1. What do you fantasize about the most? Do any of these things fall in the categories of fallen desires we discussed in chapter 1: forbidden or immoral relationships (the stuff of kings)? the love of recognition, renown, or self-exaltation in your community (the stuff of crowns)? selfish-ambition (seeking to build your own kingdoms)? the love of money and materialism (the stuff of castles)?

2. Are there disappointments in your life that you escape from in the fantasies you identified above?

3. What fears or struggles are you brewing and seething on?

4. Read Galatians 6:6–10. What corruption are you reaping from sowing sinful meditations in your life?

5. Take time to notice and write down what happens when you waste time musing on false realities and fantasies. Not only are you unable to glorify God and enjoy Him, but you are also out of commission for the kingdom. You are not advancing the kingdom through prayer, being transformed by engaging God's Word, and ministering to others. In other words, you are not staying awake to reality.

6. Read Romans 1:18–32. When we exchange the Creator for creation, we will be handed over to more sin. Can you identify more sins that have come from your misdirected meditations?

How has setting your mind on these things led you to begin seeking them, resulting in more sin?

7. Read Ephesians 1:3–14. These blessings will be fully realized in the Age to Come. But believers are able to begin enjoying these spiritual blessings today. Write down these blessings and consider ways to begin enjoying them now.

8. Start a list of your *go-to pictures*, which will begin to develop through this book. For example, if you struggle with loneliness, you may find that the vivid images of the King and His bride will be powerful tools for replacing loneliness with joy. If you are longing for a sense of true home, you may find that walking through the city of God will bless your soul. These go-to pictures will be personalized to you and help you remain awake to God's presence and His kingdom!

9. Begin practicing the powerful habit of filling your mind with God's truth through biblical meditation. Determine a time and place where you can ponder, picture, and pray God's Word. When Jade was a baby, I would meditate while rocking her to sleep. I am currently in a season of life where I like to meditate in the sauna after working out at the gym. These are just a couple of ideas. But I want to encourage you to find a time that works for you, which may require creativity in your busy life.

   Begin by *pondering* or thinking about the verse. What is God saying? *Picture* God's Word in your mind. In other words, form a picture of the truth and take time to mentally gaze upon it. These two activities will lead you to begin responding to God through prayer. You may find your-self moved to adore God, to communicate your gratitude to Him, to confess your sin, or to ask Him to help you or others in specific ways.[8] Meditating on God's Word will lead you to connect with Him on a deep level and become more like Him! Also, it may help you begin to develop this habit by starting with small amounts of time and adding more each week.

CHAPTER 3

THE SUPREME ADVENTURE OF LIFE

Some journeys take us far from home. Some adventures lead us to our destiny.

—C. S. Lewis

One evening I was sitting at the airport during a heavy snow in Rochester, Minnesota, about to board a plane to return home to winter rains in Houston. I had recently heard the gospel and was spiritually born again. My heart was filled with a newfound love for Christ, my Bible was open on my lap, and I was untangling the cords on my headphones. An older man standing nearby said, "Are you a Christian?" With the zeal of a new babe in Christ, who is proud to know the Savior of mankind, I said, "Yes! I recently heard the gospel and began a new life with Jesus."

I will never forget his response. He said, "You are in for an adventure."

It was not just *what* he said that made an impression. It was also the *way* he said it. He didn't sound like an idealist talking about a pipe dream adventure. He sounded like a man who had taken a real adventure—one that was mixed with both sufferings and glories. The brief conversation awakened a sense of sobriety and excitement at the same time, and I wondered, *What exactly is the adventure?*

I have thought about that encounter at various points in my life as God has continued to open my eyes to the epic adventure believers in Jesus Christ truly are on. I have come to see that the Christian life is far from a humdrum existence. It is a real adventure, which includes real obstacles and victories, life and death.

And all things are moving toward a destination.

SECURITY AND ADVENTURE

G. K. Chesterton said that we long for a sense of wonder and welcome in the world. We desire to adventure into this world (wonder), and yet at the same time we desire to be safe and secure (welcome).[1]

Our sense of adventure and desire for security are evident from an early age. When babes leave the womb and enter into God's world of wonder they soon begin exploring, tasting, touching, smelling, and gazing on creation. I can still remember when Jade was a toddler and captivated for the first time by the sound of thunder and the heavy downpour of rain. She stood wonderstruck in our screened-in porch as a small river began to form in our backyard, channeling in and around the tall pines. With the excitement of an explorer she proclaimed, "Out, out!"

It was not long before we were outside *without* an umbrella, allowing the current of the young river to pull us into backyard adventures—a backyard that was a miniature forest in her little eyes. Along the way, we encountered delicate white flowers flowing in the stream, a jumping frog that seemed to join in our play, the curious sensation of wet grass beneath our feet, and the exhilaration of warm water pouring over us like a glorious outdoor shower. It was thrilling to see the spirit of adventure stirred in her young soul!

But I also noticed early on that mingled with a child's innate sense of adventure is also a desire for security. And security seems to be instrumental for keeping our flame of adventure alive! One day Jade was at a playground with a child who was a little older than she was. While Jade was courageously tackling slides and rides without fear or hesitation, her friend, who initially had seemed excited to experience the adventure vicariously through Jade, would withdraw in fear when it was her turn to take the adventure for herself.

As we watched, her guardian shared with me that she had noticed that insecurity—which had been created in the little girl's life by being moved from family to family—had hindered her sense of exploration and adventure (an insecurity that Christ can no doubt heal). The scene was a vivid picture of our innate longing for both adventure and security.

But what exactly is the adventure of life? How do we take the adventure? And where do we find security to keep the flame of adventure alive? Christianity answers these questions in a compelling way.

THE SUPREME ADVENTURE: LIFE

Chesterton acknowledges that adventure is by nature something we do not plan, but something that comes to us.[2] I want to use his insight on adventure to consider the grand adventure of life that we did not plan, but that God graciously designed to come upon us.

God *originally* designed a grand adventure for humanity. In Genesis 1:1–25 we are invited to watch Him create the world. Life was full of wonder and welcome—glorious adventures in a secure world. Using the language of Chesterton, we see God create a place that truly is wild and magical—where trees grow fruit, eggs turn into birds, fruit falls in autumn, and rivers run with water.[3]

Just when we are caught up in watching God create this world of wonder, He breaks from His pattern of speaking creation into existence by the power of His Word and "then the LORD God formed the man of dust from the ground and breathed into his nostrils the breath of life, and the man became a living creature" (Gen. 2:7). God's change in creative activity causes us to pause and marvel at the obvious indication that He has a special design and care for humanity. And in Genesis 1:27–28 God defines what that special design is:

> So God created man in his own image, in the image of God he created him; male and female he created them. And God blessed them. And God said to them, "Be fruitful and multiply and fill the earth and subdue it, and have dominion over the fish of the sea and over the birds of the heavens and over every living thing that moves on the earth."

Humanity is made in God's *image* and *likeness*, and He gave us the mandate to have *dominion* over the earth and *subdue* it. These words announce the exalted role God gave humanity in creation.

The words "king" and "kingdom" are not seen in Genesis 1–3. However, as D. A. Carson has noted, king and kingdom find their roots here in a "gentle, preliminary, and anticipatory sort of way," which are then filled out later in Scripture. In Genesis 1 we see God functioning as a King who is creating, ruling, and holding people accountable, which points forward to His sovereign kingship and kingdom described in more detail later in Scripture.[4]

The King made humanity in His image to rule over the world in subjection to Him. Thus, Stephen Dempster says, "The male and female as king and queen of creation are to exercise rule over their dominion, the extent of which is the entire earth."[5] As humanity rules in obedience to God, they will represent His character, wisdom, and name throughout the world.

Imagine the grand adventure that God designed to come upon the first human couple! They were made in God's image and therefore

The first human couple was placed in Eden, a land overflowing with life, beauty, security, and abundance. They were called to cultivate and rule over the world of wonder. God designed life to be far from a humdrum existence!

fitted for a special relationship with Him and given an exalted place within creation. They were brought into a romantic, safe, and life-producing marriage. They were placed in Eden, a land overflowing with life, beauty, security, and abundance. And they were the king and queen of creation—called to explore God's wild and magical world together, cultivate it, develop it, and rule over it in a way that displayed the magnificent name of God throughout the world. God designed life to be far from a humdrum existence!

FALLEN FROM THE ADVENTURE OF LIFE

God's glory is still reflected through this created world, reminding us that we were made for something beautiful and something great. But why is the world also full of chaos, pain, and insecurity? Why have we fallen so far short of the grand life we long for? Genesis 3 reveals the answer.

God placed Adam and Eve in a world rich with blessings and pleasures, which are also connected to limits and obedience.[6] In other words, life is not a free-for-all. God is the sovereign Ruler over the world. And while Adam and Eve were free to enjoy all the pleasures of the new world and their place within it, they were to trust and obey God by living within His laws and limits. Thus, God placed one tree in the garden from which they were forbidden to eat.

In time Satan appeared in the form of a creature of the field and subtly lured Adam and Eve to disobey God. Instead of ruling over creation, they listened to the voice of their subordinate. And instead of submitting to their sovereign God, they rebelled against Him. Humanity threw off God's lordship and limits over their lives and tried to take His place as their own sovereign ruler. They erroneously thought they could take life's pleasures and do with them what they wanted. And this lie proved to be false. Humanity lost access to the tree of life, and they were exiled from their paradisiacal home with God.

LIMITS ENHANCE ADVENTURE

God made the world for our enjoyment. He has also attached laws and limits to teach us how to properly enjoy the world according to His good design. As a result, God's limits and laws do not hinder our joy. They actually make our enjoyment of life more rich and full!

G. K. Chesterton uses an example of children on a playground at the top of a cliff. "So long as there was a wall round the cliff's edge they could fling themselves into every frantic game and make the place the noisiest of nurseries." However, when you take the wall down, it will not be long before the children's play will begin to turn into timidity and fear. The lack of limits and boundaries will cause them to begin huddling together and cowering toward the middle. With the "peril of the precipice" [a cliff] in view, "their song had ceased."[7]

In a similar way, God's good laws and limits actually enable us to use our adventurous spirit in the fullest way. For example, God made us in His image to have a sacred and vibrant relationship with Him. Thus, one of His good laws or limits is that we are not to love something in creation more than Him.

SEEKING LIFE FROM THE LIFELESS

I periodically talk with my daughter about how God tells us not to love something in creation more than Him and how this good law actually enhances our joy in being human.

One day this conversation arose while I was watching Jade play with her dolls. It is so precious to watch Jade—who is alive, active, and full of personality—give animation to lifeless dolls. The contrast carried my mind to places in Scripture where God reasons with us about the foolishness of idolatry.

God is a living God, and He made us in His living image to have a special relationship with Him. Thus it is futile to worship and serve dead idols in creation instead of our Creator. When we exchange God for the lesser things He has made, we dishonor Him, because He is far greater than the things He has made. But we also belittle ourselves by worshiping (loving and serving) things in creation that are lesser things than we are!

> But our God is in the heavens; He does whatever He pleases. Their idols are silver and gold, the work of man's hands. They have mouths, but they cannot speak; they have eyes, but they cannot see; they have ears, but they cannot hear; they have noses, but they cannot smell; they have hands, but they cannot feel; they have feet, but they cannot walk; they cannot make a sound with their throat. Those who make them will become like them, everyone who trusts in them. O Israel, trust in the LORD; He is their help and their shield. (Ps. 115:3–9 NASB)

I seized the moment to reason with Jade about idolatry, saying: "Jade, isn't it amazing that God made you in His image? God is alive. Look in the mirror. You are alive, breathing, and full of personality like Him. He made you in His living likeness for a special relationship with Him. But look at your dolls. They cannot speak, see, hear, smell, or walk. So, can they do anything to help you?"

She replied with silly laughter and says, "Of course not, Mommy." I continued, "Well, then, dolls are fun to play with as toys, but wouldn't it be silly if you loved your dolls more than God and asked them to protect you, provide for you, guide you, and make you happy?" Again, she agreed with laughter at such a silly notion.

But one day, she will know that this silly notion is in fact the foolish posture of our sinful hearts. "The heart is deceitful above all things, and desperately sick; who can understand it?" (Jer. 17:9). We exchange God and look to created things such as money, houses, and mortal people to make us happy and to meet our desires.

It is a powerful and life-changing moment when we begin to grasp the significance of being made in God's image.

However, it is a powerful and life-changing moment when we begin to grasp the significance of being made in God's image. God did not make us to love and seek life in unliving things; when we do, it results in a spiritually dead life. We are made for an abundant life with a living God!

We were made to relate with God and live with Him. Therefore, apart from God, there is no point in life. Apart from God, there is no grand destination toward which we are heading. There is no epic adventure to take. As a result, many people who refuse to be reconciled to God through Jesus Christ spend their days either moaning from a deep sense of meaninglessness or making futile attempts to create a sense of adventure by doing fleeting things like traveling the world or starting new relationships and business ventures.

We have each attempted to separate the beautiful life God created from obedience to the One who made it.

But I have good news for you! This does not have to be the end of your story. God responded to humanity's fall from glory in an astonishing way. He graciously provided us with a path for salvation—one that leads us back to God through Jesus Christ and brings us into the grand adventure of new life with Him.

So let's consider how to take the one adventure that leads to the destiny we long for!

ADVENTURE-ENHANCING FENCES

1. Can you remember the awakening of adventure in your soul as a child?

2. Was there a time when your sense of adventure began to wane? What began to stifle your sense of adventure? Was there a loss of security due to sin?

3. What are some patterns in your life where you cast off God's laws and limits? What short-term pleasure do you think you will receive? How has this false pursuit of freedom resulted in bondage? (Next time you are tempted to pursue false freedom, remember the bondage you are in to discourage you from sin.)

4. Name some examples of God's gifts to us that are combined with limits that actually enhance our pleasure (e.g., marriage, consumption of food). Can you think of how obedience to God in your answers to the third question will actually make the experience of God's gifts richer?

5. How has this chapter encouraged you to pursue maximum pleasure through obedience to God versus pursuing false freedom, short-term pleasures, and shame?

CHAPTER 4

TAKING THE ADVENTURE

Let us go on and take the adventure that shall fall to us.
—C. S. Lewis

When humanity threw off God's authority, the whole world was turned upside down.[1] But God graciously responded to humanity's rebellion by giving us a Word of hope—a promise. He will restore His good design for the world. In Genesis 3:15 God announces the first gospel: "And I will put enmity between you and the woman, and between your offspring and hers; he will crush your head, and you will strike his heel" (NIV).

Do you hear dominion language running through this proclamation? God will raise up an offspring of the woman who will deliver a crushing blow to Satan and restore human dominion over the world. In 1 Corinthians 15:21–28, Paul explains that Jesus Christ is the man who will restore dominion. God will reign over the world through Jesus Christ, who is the new representative of humanity. And in Revelation 3:21 we are told even more stunning news. Jesus is creating a new humanity that will rule and reign over the new world with Him. God will restore His kingdom, which He designed to be exercised through the human race. As Stephen Dempster puts it,

God created the first human couple to rule the world with their children. They failed, were exiled, and died. They were promised a progeny who would take back what was rightfully theirs and restore wholeness and shalom to the world.[2]

Immediately following humanity's fall, God announces glorious news! A new adventure with Him has begun—the adventure of restoring God's kingdom through the offspring of Eve.

And did you notice that God has given us a source of security to compel us forward in this new adventure with Him? His promise.

God is *faithful*, and He is *able* to accomplish His good promises and plans. When we believe and trust God, we will obey Him by taking Him at His Word and following Him into the new adventure of life, the "obedience of faith" (Rom. 16:26).

THE NEW ADVENTURE THROUGH ABRAHAM

In Genesis 12, God takes a significant step forward in His plan to restore the world when He makes a covenant promise to Abram. And consider with me the new adventure of life that God graciously brought to Abram, who was a moon worshiper and wanderer (Josh. 24:2; Deut. 26:5).[3] God reveals Himself to Abram and makes a promise to do wondrous things in his life that will reverberate with wondrous blessings into the lives of others.

I love how God prefaces His covenant promise to Abram with a beautiful statement about Himself: "Fear not, Abram, I am your shield; your *reward* shall be very great" (Gen. 15:1). God is real, He is our great Reward, and He is a generous Rewarder of those who diligently seek Him (Heb. 11:6, 26). Listen carefully to the echoes of the blessings God bestowed on the first human couple that God transfers to a new humanity He is going to create through Abram:

> Then Abram fell on his face. And God said to him, "Behold, my covenant is with you, and you shall be the father of a multitude of nations. No longer shall your name be called Abram, but your name shall be Abraham, for I have made you the father of a multitude of nations. I will make you exceedingly fruitful, and I will make you into nations, and kings shall come from you. And I will establish my covenant between me and you and your offspring after you throughout their generations for an everlasting covenant, to be God to you and to your offspring after you. And I will give to you and to your offspring after you the land of your sojournings, all the land of Canaan, for an everlasting possession, and I will be their God." (Gen. 17:3–8)

Do you hear the echoes of God's original design for humanity in Genesis 1–2 reverberating through God's promise to Abraham?

God blessed Adam and Eve to be fruitful. Now God tells Abraham that He will make him a fruitful father of nations.

God gave Adam and Eve the royal mandate to rule over the earth in subjection to Him as His representatives. Now God tells Abraham that kings shall come from him.

God's plan was to undo the effects of the fall through the family of Abraham, from which Jesus eventually came. When Sarai was promised she would be the mother of nations and kings, God changed her name to Sarah, which means "princess" (Gen. 17:15–16).

The realm God told Adam and Eve to rule over in subjection to Him was the whole earth. Now God tells Abraham that He will give him and his new royal family an everlasting land.

God made Adam and Eve in His image to walk with Him. And God concludes His promise to Abraham saying that He will be the God of the new people He will create through this man.

Abraham, whose family once worshiped the moon, will become the father of a royal family created by the One who made the moon.

God is re-creating the world to its Edenic glory! And Abraham has found himself graciously chosen by God to play a significant role within God's plan. Abraham, whose family once worshiped the moon, will become the father of a royal family created by the One who made the moon. Abraham, a wanderer, will inherit an everlasting land.

Sarai, who was once a barren woman, was given the new name Sarah, and she would "produce heirs for the throne of [the new] creation."[4] And we see that Abraham and Sarah took the new adventure of life with God by trusting His promises and obeying His Word (Heb. 6:13–14; 17–18). Hebrews 6:17 says God's purpose is unchangeable and guaranteed. God presented Abraham with a future full of hope, and God is calling us to join this adventure by repenting of our sin and beginning a new life with Jesus Christ. We should be encouraged that the same God who called Abraham and was faithful to him is calling us and directing our lives today.

A FAR BETTER ADVENTURE

After graduating from college, I moved to Houston to begin my last venture apart from God before Jesus graciously interrupted my life with the gospel. My new course was set in the direction of seeking romance and wonder under the city lights of Houston and in the glittering fabrics of a career in the fashion industry. The energy of the city seemed to match the energy of my own, and so I dove headlong into my career, a new culture of godless relationships, and carousing downtown on the weekends.

But eight months after my arrival, I experienced something similar to Abraham. God called me through the gospel to leave my life of idolatry behind. There was wrestling in my soul over the call to leave my life of sin behind, but when the gospel continued to be preached over me, something powerful and supernatural happened. God opened the eyes of my heart to see the light of Christ's beauty and majesty (2 Cor. 4:4–6). I became like a woman struck with love at first sight. And all the other attractions around me began to fade in their luster.

My change of course was nothing I planned or dreamt up on my own. And I certainly didn't have the moral fortitude to begin a self-righteous and religious journey. Instead, my life changed course because the sail of my affections was swept up by the wind of God's supreme beauty and seeing Him as my greater Reward. After responding to the gracious call of God to leave behind my life of sin, I went on to end my godless relationship with my boyfriend. God quickly connected me with His family—the church—and began transforming my life in dramatic ways.

Years later, I still find myself overwhelmed with gratitude

that God interrupted my journeys and brought me into the epic adventure of new life with Him.

What about you? Are you still sailing on godless ventures? May today mark the beginning of your new life with Christ. Like Abraham, Sarah, and many others who have gone before you, take the step of faith to leave behind your life of sin. As C. S. Lewis observed, there are far, far greater things in the Age to Come than anything you will leave behind.[5]

A NEW DYNASTY THROUGH DAVID

It is fascinating to watch God's faithfulness to His promise. God did bless Abraham and Sarah. They were fruitful, and their offspring began the nation of Israel. In time, God raised up a king from Abraham's descendants, namely, David. Like Abraham, David trusted God's Word and obeyed Him, leading to many adventures with God. He defeated Goliath, overcame the persecution of King Saul, and was raised up by God from the pastures to become the prince over God's people.

It would seem that these ventures were enough for one man's lifetime. But God still had more stunning plans in store for David—worldwide plans, eternal plans, plans that would be a blessing to many.

By the time we arrive at 2 Samuel 7:1, God has raised up David to be the prince over God's people. God has granted David rest from wars with the nation's surrounding enemies. Therefore, David is living at peace in his royal house or palace. And here we see David's deep love for God once again. David was bothered by the fact he was living in a palace while the ark of God was still dwelling in a tent. Therefore, David asks if he can build a house for God. God's response is stunning—He says no, you cannot build a house for Me, but I will build a house for you! And this house is no ordinary house, as declared through the prophet Nathan:

> "'The LORD declares to you that the LORD will make you a house. When your days are fulfilled and you lie down with your fathers, I will raise up your offspring after you, who shall come from your body, and I will establish his kingdom. He shall build a house for my name, and I will establish the throne of his kingdom forever. I will be to him a father, and he shall be to me a son. . . . And your house and your kingdom shall be made sure forever before me. Your throne shall be established forever.'" In accordance with all these words, and in accordance with all this vision, Nathan spoke to David. (2 Sam. 7:11–14, 16–17)

Did you catch that? David asks God if he can build a house for Him. David means a physical house—a building, a temple. And God says no, but *I* will build *you* a house. God is clearly not saying that He is going to build David a physical house or building to live in.

The passage begins by telling us that David is already living in his royal house. "Now when the king lived in his house and the LORD had given him rest from all his surrounding enemies, the king said to Nathan the prophet, 'See now, I dwell in a house of cedar, but the ark of God dwells in a tent'" (vv. 1–2). So what house is God referring to?

GOD'S GREATER PLANS

God's generous nature is breathtaking once again! David loves God and wants to honor Him. And God responds by showing His love to David in a far greater and eternal way. God is going to build a house, meaning a royal house—a dynasty of kings through David. And God says this dynasty or royal family will be an everlasting kingdom: "your house and your kingdom shall be made sure *forever* before me" (v. 16). Jesus is the ultimate fulfillment of God's promise to David. And as we will see, those who are united to Jesus by faith will participate in these promises as well!

God has many kingdom adventures for all who love and seek Him. But like David, there may be times when we have a sincere desire to honor God and express our love for Him in a specific way, yet God says no. When we submit to Jesus as our King, we find that He has specific kingdom works for us (Eph. 2:10). And sometimes our own agenda does not align with His plans for us.

> **A person who is spiritually born again by grace through faith is brought into the new royal family that God is creating. We are destined for indescribable, eternal adventures with the King!**

Surrendering our own desires and plans when they come into conflict with God's should not cause us to fall into despair. God is gloriously good and rejoices to do good to His people (Jer. 32:41). We will discuss this in more detail in the pages to come. But for now, let me just say that a person who is spiritually born again by grace through faith is brought into the new royal family that God is creating through

David's Son, Jesus Christ. As a result, we are destined for indescribable, eternal adventures with the King!

BEYOND OUR DREAMS

It is just a matter of time until believers step into the fullness of joy in the presence of our King and eternal pleasures with Him in the Age to Come. And I am certain that none of us will then look back with disappointment over unfulfilled dreams in this fleeting and perishing world. This should be encouraging for any who are struggling with the disappointment of unfulfilled dreams. And it should free us to serve the Lord with joy and excellence in the lot He has given us as we eagerly anticipate the eternal day to come.

One afternoon I was mopping the floor and feeling discouraged about an unfulfilled dream. But as I lifted my heart up to the Lord in prayer, He filled it with a time of life-changing worship. As I was praying, I was reminded of something thrilling. Yes, it is true that what I wanted God to give me was not in the picture of my life on that day, but He reminded me of *who* was standing gloriously with me—namely, Jesus!

My disappointment began causing me to fall into the slumber of sin, if you will, but God graciously awakened me back to a bright reality where He is always with me. My heart was filled with deep love and intimate appreciation for my King. And I realized, *it's okay. It's okay when we don't get all our dreams, because we have Him. And oh, how thrilling it is to go where He leads us because we are with Him.* I turned on some music and began to worship. And let me just tell you, it was the best time I have ever had mopping my floor.

May your heart find rest in the fellowship of believers who

sometimes hear God say no to our dreams, but are then reminded that He has far, far better dreams in store for us. As Christians, we are blessed to know that Jesus is the King. He is on His throne and leading us on kingdom adventures now. But there is much more of the adventure yet to come—adventures we will take in a new world for ages upon ages!

PROMISES THROUGH THE PROPHETS

The significance of the Davidic covenant cannot be overstated. The prophecies and promises concerning the kings, crowns, kingdom, and castles to come through Jesus Christ flow from this promise made to David. Furthermore, the promise that God will set a son of David on the eternal throne and establish an eternal kingdom became the hope of God's people.[6]

When David had served God's purpose in his own generation, he died, and his throne went to his son Solomon. Though Solomon starts well, he does not end well, revealing that he is not the son God was ultimately referring to in His promise to David. Solomon and the nation's future kings continue to fall short of God's character and ways. And due to the sin of the nation, God eventually exiled His people from the Promised Land.

During this period, God graciously speaks through prophets to encourage His exiled people that He has not forgotten His promise to David. In fact, the name of the prophet Zechariah means, "the LORD remembers." Our God is so kind! He provides us with pictures of hope concerning the glorious destiny of God's people. God gave many of these promises to Israel during their time of exile as a means of encouragement, so also God teaches us to take hold of these promises during our seasons of suffering.

> So we do not lose heart. Though our outer self is wasting away, our inner self is being renewed day by day. For this light momentary affliction is preparing for us an eternal weight of glory beyond all comparison, as we look not to the things that are seen but to the things that are unseen. For the things that are seen are transient, but the things that are unseen are eternal. (2 Cor. 4:16–18)

Many of our ventures through this world involve suffering. I hesitate to even describe such seasons as an adventure because that word can sound unsympathetic and shallow. But I am reminded of the epic story of The Lord of the Rings. In this trilogy, the fate of all of civilization rests on the results of a grand adventure. Powerful forces are involved, great matters of life and death. Heroism and courage are needed to persevere to the end.

In a similar way, many times in this fallen world, suffering and tragedy come upon us. All of a sudden we turn a corner in life and the word "adventure" no longer seems fitting. We feel like cowering back, because moving forward in the will of God looks frightening. It is especially important to continue to move forward during these times, because failure to persevere through hardship may be an indicator that a person is an unbeliever (Luke 8:13). But God brings us through these tribulations and conforms us more into His image when we trust Him and hold fast to His Word.

When I was a young single woman—shortly after beginning my new life with Christ and still young in my faith—my father received a diagnosis of cancer. The days were dark, my confusion was high, and my heart was low. I took a leave of absence from work to return to the land of my roots and be with the man I dearly loved as his body began to deteriorate.

One evening at twilight, I was standing on the deck of our house overlooking an open field of dead brown grass, which seemed to reflect the vacancy of my life. The sky was giving way to gray tones and black shadows. My breath left a trail of steam against the cold winter air. And though everyone else had taken refuge in the warmth of the house, I remained outside because the frigidity felt good against the hot questions that were confusing my mind.

Thoughts began to swirl in all directions: Is God angry with me? Is my faith lacking? Perhaps this "Christian thing" is not real. Perhaps I should not continue to follow Christ. I could call my friends, who live a few hours away, and go back to my old ways, which might give me some instant relief from my distress.

But when I contemplated going back to my old sinful ways, something strange took place. Each backward path seemed so filthy and unfulfilling after having tasted the purity and joy of walking with Christ. The temptation to depart from Jesus was silenced by one acknowledgment: after experiencing His greatness and sweetness, where would I go? I could not think of another place! I returned to my house still broken and confused but ready to endure the dark night of my soul with Christ (John 6:67–68).

In the days that followed, God introduced me to the book of Revelation and His glorious promises through the prophets. As I sat by my father's side in the last few months of his life, reading about the end times and the new world to come, it was both mysteriously sad and sweet.

God's promises of the new world to come through the words of the prophets gave me a great deal of strength to continue moving through this tribulation in Christ with hope and courage. Looking back, I can see that God used that suffering to forge me more into His likeness. He impressed upon me the fleeting nature of this perishing world and began to set my eyes on the glorious new world to come.

God graciously spoke prophetic words of encouragement to His exiled people, assuring them that He will be true to His promises. And these promises

> **By the time we come to the close of the Old Testament, God's people are eagerly anticipating the coming King who will usher in the kingdom of God.**

are treasures for us when we travel through hardships as well. By the time we come to the close of the Old Testament, God's people are eagerly anticipating the coming King who will usher in the kingdom of God.

THE SON OF NOBLE BIRTH

The New Testament begins with cosmic hype about the birth of a child. Genealogies are traced to show that this child is from the line of Abraham and David. A wicked king becomes jealous

71

of the child and is given over to murderous fear. Wise men begin their journey to bring gifts to the Child from afar, following the star that has settled and is shining over the place where He was. And the angel Gabriel appeared to a virgin named Mary to announce the miraculous conception, identity, and destiny of the Child:

> "Behold, you will conceive in your womb and bear a son, and you shall call his name Jesus. He will be great and will be called the Son of the Most High. And the Lord God will give to him the throne of his father David, and he will reign over the house of Jacob forever, and of his kingdom there will be no end." (Luke 1:31–33)

Gabriel's announcement is filled with the language of 2 Samuel 7. Jesus Christ is the Son of David who will sit on the eternal throne. He will establish, sustain, and rule over a kingdom that will have no end. And we see that all the messianic promises throughout the Old Testament are fulfilled in Jesus Christ!

Through the Gospels we see Jesus live the perfect moral life that we failed to live. He died on the cross to pay the penalty for our sins that we could not pay, and to defeat Satan, an enemy we could not defeat. He rose from the dead, conquering sin and death. And He ascended into heaven where He sits on His throne at the right hand of the Father. All authority in heaven and earth has been given to Jesus. And He will return to execute justice, remove wickedness from the land, and restore the world to its Edenic glory.

But before that time, Jesus is advancing His kingdom in the hearts of people through the preaching of the gospel. And this is where we currently stand on God's kingdom calendar today. We will unpack how to pursue lives that are marked by the kingdom of God in the pages to come. But first, let me conclude by summing up the end of the story.

Revelation 11:15 gives us a glimpse of our King's future return, when His enemies are put under His feet and the whole world comes under His good lordship: "The kingdom of the world has become the kingdom of our Lord and of his Christ, and he shall reign forever and ever." At that time we will see Jesus do something that should not be surprising at this point in the biblical story because we have been told about it since the beginning of time.

But it continues to be stunning news, regardless of how many times we have heard it. Jesus will restore the world to its Edenic state and lead His people to regain the royal status and dominion God bestowed on humanity when He originally created the world:[7] "They will need no light of lamp or sun, for the Lord God will be their light, and they will reign forever and ever" (Rev. 22:5).

God is gracious, and He has designed a great and glorious salvation. So how do we begin this new life adventure? And if we have already begun the adventure, how do we continue on it with devotion and joy?

THE SUPREME ADVENTURE OF BEING BORN "AGAIN"

When humanity threw off God's good authority, we fell from the adventure of life that He originally designed to come upon us. However, there is one word that fills our sails with new wonder and security. And that word is "again." The supreme adventure is being born *again*. In John 3:3 Jesus says, "Truly, truly, I say to you, unless one is born again he cannot see the kingdom of God."

How can a woman be born again? God causes a woman to be spiritually born again by grace through faith in the gospel. God is awakening men, women, and children from the slumber of sin by giving them new life through the gospel!

Adventures in Repentance

God showed His great love for us by giving His Son, Jesus Christ, to live the perfect moral life that we could not live, to die on our behalf to pay the penalty for our sin. After Jesus died and was buried, He rose again to bring us into new life with Him, thereby conquering sin and death on our behalf. This is the gospel or good news! When a woman hears the good news of God's gracious gift of salvation and believes by repenting of her sin and submitting to Jesus Christ, the adventure of new life has begun. "The time is fulfilled, and the kingdom of God is at hand; repent and believe in the gospel" (Mark 1:15).

Repentance is powerful and necessary for taking the new life adventure. Simply stated, repentance is a change of mind. Repentance moves us to turn away from our godless pursuits and turn to Jesus as our King. When we repent of our sin and put our trust in Jesus, we begin to discover that the Christian life is far from a humdrum existence. God rescues us from the dominion of darkness and transfers us into the kingdom of His beloved Son (Col. 1:13 NIV). And we begin a new life with Christ that leads to the glorious destination we all long for.

Adventures in Obedience

The way we continue the adventure with Jesus is to read His Word and apply it to our lives. Repentance is when we give up our plans for how our adventure will go and start trusting God to guide us on the adventure He has for us. And each time we walk in obedience to His commands, we set sail on new adventures with Him.

I wish we had more space to talk about all the adventures that come from reading and obeying God's Word. There are grand adventures that come upon us when we apply Christ's ways to our relationships, churches, the stewardship of our gifts and talents for Christ's kingdom, using our resources in generous ways, living for others, and much, much more. We will talk about some of these throughout the remaining pages of this book, but for now I hope to have inspired you to begin seeing obedience to God as the glorious path to the epic adventure of new life with Christ.

TAKING THE NEW ADVENTURE

1. Have you begun the adventure of life with God by repenting of your sin and trusting in Jesus for salvation? If not, I am thrilled to have the opportunity to invite you to receive Christ. Please read Romans 10:8–10.

2. If your answer to the first question is yes, then I would like to invite you to take time to write down, savor, and worship Jesus for the different adventures He has led you on through your obedience to His Word in the past.

3. Are there areas of disobedience in your life that are displeasing to God and causing you to miss out on taking kingdom adventures with Him today? For example, if you are not in fellowship with other Christians, you are missing out on adventures in relationships. If you are not giving your resources to kingdom work, then you are missing out on adventures in the expansion of God's kingdom. How are you inspired to make changes in your life today?

3. Read Hebrews 6:13–20. What was the anchor of Abraham's soul that compelled him to embark on such an amazing adventure with God? From the same passage, what is the anchor for you?

4. Find some promises of God that relate to your area of fear, insecurity, and disobedience. How do God's promises give you security to take new kingdom adventures with Him by the obedience of faith?

PART 2

THE KING
AND HIS BRIDE

CHAPTER 5

A KING WORTH LIVING FOR

You make known to me the path of life; in your presence there is fullness of joy; at your right hand are pleasures forevermore.

—Psalm 16:11

A dear friend of my family grew up in the Kingdom of Saudi Arabia. One night we were having dinner with Jon and his wife when he asked how my writing was coming along. After sharing with them the vision for this book, Jon replied, "One of the challenges you are going to face is helping Western thinkers grasp the rich concepts of king and kingdom. It is not natural for people raised on the principles of a democratic republic to understand the ins and outs of a kingdom, much less the importance of its king."

Jon began to share his personal story of coming to understand more fully the concepts of king and kingdom while growing up as an American citizen under a monarch. During their time in Saudi Arabia, Jon's father was working on a large construction project and learned that the king would be visiting the project during its final phase of construction. A local citizen had been chosen to carry incense in front of the king as he walked through the facility.

Being a young Western-thinking individualist, Jon scoffed at the notion and said, "If I were a king, I would never make one of my subjects do that for me." To Jon's surprise, his father responded, "You don't get it, son. The day that a man gets to serve his king will be the biggest day of his life; he will never be the same." In that moment Jon began to realize how significant it is for a common man to receive an audience with his king and that to serve the king would be a tremendous honor.

Jon explained it would be highly unlikely for the king to ever visit an ordinary person who, for example, lives in an apartment and goes about his daily business of selling fish in a seaside province. The citizen, of course, knows the king. He has heard famous stories about the king's father. He read tales of the country's greatness and sang of its might. And he even has a painting of the king in his home and another one hanging in his fish stall.

Many of us do not fully grasp the rich realities of Christ's kingship and kingdom. We fall short of living in wonder of the gospel that grants us an audience with the King of kings.

But the common man going about his daily life would have no expectation of receiving an audience with the king. And if for some reason the man received an invitation to do something for the king—such as give him a fish from his stall—his life would be changed forever. He would no longer be seen as a "common man" among his neighbors. Instead, he would be known as "the man who once served the king."

As I listened to Jon, I realized he was right. Many of us do not fully grasp the rich realities of Christ's kingship and kingdom. As a result, we fall short of living in wonder of the gospel that grants us an audience with the King of kings and the honor that comes from being citizens of His kingdom who are given gifts and roles to serve Him. Thus, I am excited to begin wrapping our minds around the kingship of Jesus Christ and the glories of His kingdom in order to lead us into higher levels of wonder and gratitude toward Him.

THE SUPREME KING

As we begin this venture together, I think it is fitting to be honest with you by sharing that this has been the hardest chapter to write. How do you describe a King who is so supreme that the destiny of the world will be shaped by who He is? Consider this: a king determines what his kingdom will be like and therefore what life will be like for those under his reign. A wicked ruler will create a kingdom and society that is ruthless, oppressive, and terrifying.

But Jesus is a good and perfect King. As a result, His kingdom is full of glories and rich blessings for those who live under His rule. Jesus is also supreme above all kings. His dominion will not merely extend throughout a city or nation; but rather, it will extend to the ends of the earth! Therefore, as we enter into a prophetic picture of our coming King, I want to focus our eyes on a specific point; namely, all the glorious features of the Age to Come that we will discuss throughout the remaining chapters exist because of who the King of the world is. And for this reason, the citizens of Christ's kingdom will become a society that lives in praise and worship for our King!

PSALMS THAT POINT TO JESUS

One thing many of us admire about David is that he had a dynamic love and zeal for God. We see an expression of this when he was installed as the king over Israel and began writing psalms and taking initiatives to lead people into the praise and worship of God as well. But some of the psalms David and others wrote are prophetic, meaning that God inspired them—"For no prophecy was ever produced by the will of man, but men spoke from God as they were carried along by the Holy Spirit" (2 Peter 1:21)—and He inspired these psalms about Jesus long before Jesus came to fulfill them (Isa. 42:9; Heb. 1:1–4).

Jesus acknowledged that the Old Testament pointed forward to Him, saying, "Everything written about me in the Law of Moses and the Prophets and the *Psalms* must be fulfilled" (Luke 24:44). The church refers to the psalms that point forward to Jesus as messianic, and these messianic psalms provide us with previews of Jesus' death, resurrection, ascension, enthronement, and kingdom.[1] The Holy Spirit helps us identify messianic psalms by directly applying some of the psalms to Jesus in the New Testament. Thus, we see that the Holy Spirit inspired human authors and gave them previews of the coming King and His kingdom to share with us. So let's follow them into their worship!

ENTHUSIASM FOR THE COMING KING

In Psalm 45:1 we are introduced to a psalmist who has been inspired by God to share a message with us. The psalmist is inspired by a good word that has made his heart burst with joy: "My heart overflows with a pleasing theme; I address my verses to the king; my tongue is like the pen of a ready scribe."

Oh, how uplifting is the psalmist's enthusiasm! We are in desperate need of good messages today. The current events and news become disheartening, and much of what we see in movies and on social media is morally dark and discouraging. And our own lives are filled with trials and afflictions.

As a result we can find ourselves consumed with discouraging news, events, and encounters with people, which weigh our hearts down more and more. If we are not careful, our *perspective* of life can grow dimmer and dimmer. Therefore, good news is not only possible to find in the Bible, but it is necessary for us to dwell on: "Anxiety weighs down the heart, but a kind word cheers it up" (Prov. 12:25 NIV).

So what is the good word that the psalmist is brimming over with enthusiasm to share? He is inspired to think about the coming King from David's line who will fulfill God's glorious promises to His people! By now, we have seen that God's promises to Abraham and David are filled with the concepts of kings, crowns, and kingdoms. There-

We will realize in that moment that Jesus is everything we have ever desired. Can you imagine?

fore, we should not be surprised to find that all these things are in this prophetic picture of the Age to Come.

You may, however, be surprised to learn that the setting for Psalm 45 is a royal wedding between a Hebrew king and a foreign princess.[2] But like other messianic psalms, it has another meaning that extends beyond the original wedding celebration to a greater and higher celebration.[3] This is what C. S. Lewis refers to as the "second meanings in the psalms."[4] What's the clue? Look at who the groom is in verse 6! "Your throne, O God, is forever and ever. The scepter of your kingdom is a scepter of uprightness."

This verse is a reference to the covenant God made with David in 2 Samuel 7:13 to set His Son on an eternal throne. And Hebrews 1:8–9 confirms that Jesus is the King referred to in Psalm 45:6. Jesus is the all-glorious King who will conquer the world and reign with His beautiful bride, the church, by His side. Let's focus our eyes on the King, who is no doubt the central and most captivating feature in the picture.

THE MOST HANDSOME OF MEN—A GRACIOUS KING

The first splendor we notice about the King is that He is far superior to all men, "You are the most handsome of the sons of men" (Ps. 45:2). Now, I don't know about you, but my heart is already beginning to pound. I need to calm down because we are just getting started! Psalm 45 is filled with physical language describing what the King looks like, sounds like, and even smells like. All the descriptive language certainly provokes us to anticipate the thrilling fact that believers in Jesus Christ will one day live with Him face to face forever! And when we see Jesus, we will see a Man of human superiority.

We will realize in that moment that Jesus is everything we have ever desired. Can you imagine? All the temptations to seek romantic adventures in this fallen world, to find someone who will ultimately fulfill us, will at last come to an end when we stand in the presence of the One for whom we are made. Our love for Him will erupt to the highest measure of love it can. And our affections will seat Him on the throne of our hearts, never again to be threatened by lesser rivals. This is your destiny, believer in Jesus Christ!

Closely following the attractive nature of the King, we are told that His speech is full of grace. "You are the most handsome of the sons of men; grace is poured upon your lips; therefore God has blessed you forever" (v. 2). I do not think the connection between Christ's gracious speech (which overflows from His gracious heart) and His handsome appearance is random.

I know a woman whose husband struggles with anger, which often overflows from his heart into sharp and harsh words toward his wife and children. But shortly after working to replace his anger with gentle and gracious words, his daughter began calling him her "handsome daddy." No one had ever heard the little girl describe her daddy that way before. What was the connection?

Many men are great and powerful. But apart from goodness and kindness, such men can be terrifying and harsh. God is all-powerful and great, which is certainly attractive. But His beauty is primarily seen in His goodness—the fact that He uses His power and greatness in good ways.[5] Thus, there seems to be a fitting flow of thought. We see that the King is the most handsome of men and grace is poured upon His lips.

The King's gracious speech is the first distinct aspect of His beauty described in this psalm. And perhaps this will be one of the first features we'll notice about Jesus when we see Him face to face. In other words, our first impression of the King may very well be His graciousness. This character trait was recognized early on by people who lived during Christ's earthly ministry as well.

When Jesus began His ministry, news began to spread about His teaching. One day He came to Nazareth to teach in the synagogue. You can only imagine the eagerness and interest people had, wondering which passage of Scripture this up-and-coming teacher would expound upon. Jesus unrolled the scroll of the prophet Isaiah and read:

> "The Spirit of the Lord is upon me, because he has anointed me to proclaim good news to the poor. He has sent me to proclaim liberty to the captives and recovering of sight to the blind, to set at liberty those who are oppressed, to proclaim the year of the Lord's favor." (Luke 4:18–19)

After He read Isaiah's centuries-old prophecy, people's eyes were fixed on Him and their ears were alert. His exegesis was simple and yet so profound that it moved the crowd to amazement. "Today this Scripture has been fulfilled in your hearing," Jesus told them (Luke 4:21). The point would have been clear to His Jewish audience. Jesus announced that He is the long-awaited Messiah who has come to usher in the kingdom of God.[6]

What captured the people's attention—other than the obvious fact that He was declaring Himself to be the long-awaited King? His gracious speech! "And all spoke well of him and marveled at the *gracious words* that were coming from his mouth" (v. 22). Jesus announced that He is the long-awaited King and had come to do incredibly gracious works in the lives of sinful people—works that will save them, build them up, and give them a rich future with Him.

The first point we need to note about the Age to Come is that all the prophecies we see scattered throughout the Bible concerning the kings, queens, castles, and crowns to come flow from this character trait of our King. He has a gracious heart, which overflows into gracious words and works on our behalf. Grace is getting something undeserved. We do not deserve to be reconciled back to the King and to be restored to all these secondary gifts. But this King loves being good even to those who do not deserve it. Therefore, He has designed salvation to be a gift of grace (Eph. 2:8–9). And how does He want us to respond? By cherishing, celebrating, and praising Him as our gracious King (Eph. 1:6, 12, 14).

> **God will glorify His people who glorify Him, making us sparkle like crown jewels.**

Here is just one example of how the glories of the Age to Come flow directly from the King's good heart, which will create a society that loves to praise its King. Zechariah 9:16–17 says, "On that day the LORD their God will save them, as the flock of his people; for like the jewels of a crown they shall shine on his land. *For how great is his goodness, and how great his beauty!*"

God will glorify His people who glorify Him, making us sparkle like crown jewels. And He will do this, not because we deserve it, but because He is beautifully good and gracious!

THE WARRIOR KING

The next feature of the King that will awaken great enthusiasm within us is that He is a mighty and victorious warrior. Does this contradict the King's gracious nature? Let's examine how Christ's virtues neither compete with one another nor water each other down. Instead the bold character traits of the King are held vibrantly together:[7]

> Gird your sword on your thigh, O mighty one, in your splendor and majesty! In your majesty ride out victoriously

for the cause of truth and meekness and righteousness; let your right hand teach you awesome deeds! Your arrows are sharp in the heart of the king's enemies; the peoples fall under you. (Ps. 45:3–5)

The King is a mighty warrior who will return to conquer those who refuse to repent of their sin and submit to Him. And when He returns, the King will ride forth for the cause of truth and the meekness of righteousness. Let's look at the connection between humility and righteousness.

Deuteronomy 17:18–20 describes the qualifications for a king who represents God. A king was not to assume the throne and begin forming his own agenda for the kingdom. Instead, the king was to be a student of the King's law. He was to read, copy, and obey God's law carefully. By doing so, the king would take on the righteous character traits of God and reflect God's image throughout the kingdom. And the king's humility before the Lord would result in obedience to God.

The king's heart would not be lifted up above God's law, causing him to think he is not subjected to God's Word or limits. And his humility would also result in righteous living toward God's people because his heart would not be lifted up over his brothers whereby he would begin to oppress them. Thus, the king was to be humble before the Lord and by doing so, he would be righteous before God and righteous toward his brothers.[8]

Now think back with me to the garden of Eden. Adam and Eve were the king and queen of creation. But they became arrogant, throwing off God's limits and laws. They wanted to take God's place as the ultimate authority over their own lives and to have their kingdom, crowns, and castles apart from Him. But when Jesus, the second Adam, came to earth, we see a King who is quite different!

Though this may sound odd, one of my favorite accounts in the Gospels is Satan's temptation of Jesus in the wilderness (Matt. 4:1–11). This sacred moment in history has always caused me to erupt with victorious worship, because it is a showdown between Jesus Christ, the God-man, and Satan. The temptation of Christ was a cosmic replay of Adam and Eve in the garden of Eden! Like he did Adam, Satan tempted Jesus to seek His kingship and kingdom apart from the Father. But Jesus did not want anything apart from the Father. Therefore, He did not allow His heart to become arrogant and lifted up above God's law. Instead, He remained humble and righteous.

Adam, the first representative of man, lost dominion due to arrogance and unrighteousness. But Jesus, the new representative of humanity, reclaimed dominion by the humility of righteousness (1 Cor. 15:21–28). As a result, there will be no end to Jesus' throne! Through this account we see Jesus' human superiority once again. He is not only the most gracious of men. He is also the victorious warrior who defeated Satan in the wilderness temptation, which was a preview of Christ's decisive victory that would be won on the cross. Jesus sent Satan into retreat and "Jesus advanced as the divine warrior, the God of battles who fights on behalf of his people and for their salvation (cf. Ex. 15:3; Ps. 98:1). His triumph demonstrated that 'the kingdom of God is near' and the messianic conflict had begun."[9]

Jesus came the first time to defeat sin, Satan, and death. Now He is giving people time to receive His gracious gift of salvation. But when He returns, He will ride forth for the cause of truth and the humility of righteousness to conquer those who refuse to repent of their sin and submit to Him!

These character traits of Jesus will give birth to beautiful features of life in the Age to Come. When Jesus returns, He will conquer His enemies. Justice will roll down like a river and righteousness like an ever-flowing stream (Amos 5:24). Then, Zechariah 9:10 tells us that Jesus will remove chariots, warhorses, and battle bows. In other words, He will establish peace to the ends of the world and be known as the Prince of Peace. The King will comfort His people as a mother comforts her child, and He will establish a government of peace that exists to nurture its people (Isa. 9:6; 66:13; Rev. 21:4).

AN UPRIGHT AND JOYFUL KING

Jesus Christ is the most excellent of men. And He is also God. Jesus is the God-man who will rule on the worldwide throne:

> Your throne, O God, is forever and ever. The scepter of your kingdom is a scepter of uprightness; you have loved righteousness and hated wickedness. Therefore God, your God, has anointed you with the oil of gladness beyond your companions. (Ps. 45:6–7)

Another splendor of the King that will awaken great enthusiasm in our hearts for His return is that He is God and He will rule the world forever in uprightness. This is good news! Sin and wickedness ruin everything. So many good things in life go bad because of sin. One day I was ministering to a newlywed who had been so excited to marry her fiancé and begin a new life together.

However, her enjoyment of this beautiful gift from God came crashing down when she walked into a room and found her husband engaging in pornography after they said, "I do."

Jesus will never fail us by turning to wickedness and breaking our hearts. He loves righteousness and hates wickedness (v. 7). Therefore, He is going to rule over the world in uprightness forever. We see many pictures of the Age to Come as a place of righteousness and exultant joy. For example, we are told that God will rejoice and dance over His people with loud singing (Zeph. 3:17).

The King is righteous and joyful; therefore, He will create a kingdom of righteous and joyful people!

We are told that the King will give His people "the oil of gladness instead of mourning, the garment of praise instead of a faint spirit; that they may be called oaks of righteousness, the planting of the LORD, that he may be glorified" (Isa. 61:3). Did you notice the link in this verse between the oil of gladness and righteous living? The King is righteous and joyful; therefore, He will create a kingdom of righteous and joyful people!

THE ROYAL WEALTH OF THE KING

After providing us with a prophetic picture of our King to awaken great enthusiasm in us for His return, the Holy Spirit describes the King's royal robes, glorious palaces, and the music in the air: "Your robes are fragrant with myrrh and aloes and cassia. From ivory palaces stringed instruments make you glad" (Ps. 45:8). The mention of temporal beauties surrounding the King echo the Edenic beauty and abundance that Jesus will restore, which we will discuss more in chapter 11, "Walking through the City of God."

AN AUDIENCE WITH THE KING

One would expect an exalted King to announce His coming to the lofty people of the earth. But instead He came to seek and save lowly sinners and to lead us back to glory. It is crazy that anyone would refuse such a good and glorious King. But why do we? The answer is simple. Fallen humanity does not want to submit to God as our Lord. We inherited the sin nature of our first human parents. And we are radically autonomous. We want to be the sovereign lord over our own lives, building our own kingdoms, and pursuing our own agendas.

But Jesus is a glorious King. He speaks gracious words to us through the gospel—inviting us to receive Him as our King and the gift of His kingdom (Matt. 22:1–14). The question left for us to answer, then, is whether we will respond to the invitation and come to the banquet or ignore it and stay in our sin. Christ's grace extends past our borders of comprehension. The high King of heaven does not only grant us an audience with Him, He will take believers to be His bride and make us part of His new royal family!

ADVENTURES WITH THE KING

Psalm 45 is a preview of the glorious Age to Come, which is only partially realized now in the lives of those who have been united to Jesus Christ by faith. But our adventure with our King has already begun. So let's consider how to experience our King and take kingdom adventures with Him now!

1. *Connecting with the Most Excellent of Men*: In 1 Peter 1:8–9, we are reminded that even though we cannot presently see Jesus face to face, we believe in Him and are filled with love for our Lord of glory. How do we experience love for Jesus without seeing Him now? The word for "love" in this verse refers to "a love that is called out of one's heart by the preciousness of the one loved."[10] When a man or a woman believes in Jesus Christ, God opens the eyes of their heart to see Him (2 Cor. 4:4–6). When we see Jesus with spiritual vision, we cannot help but love Him! Therefore, when we feel lonely, we can remind ourselves that this lonely day or difficult season will not last forever; we can pick up our Bibles and ask the most handsome of Men to connect with us as we relate with Him through His Word. And He is faithful to show up! How can you put this truth into practice this week?

2. *Awakening Enthusiasm for the King*: Peter says that believers can experience inexpressible joy in this life, even in the midst of the many sufferings (1 Peter 1:8–9). I love the way Peter describes a believer's joy as "inexpressible" or too deep for words. When we set our eyes on the coming King and His glorious kingdom to come, we will experience inexpressible joy and enthusiasm like David and the psalmist. Start developing the habit of meditating on portraits of our coming King and His kingdom before going to bed, instead of watching television or engaging in social media, and watch your perspective and enthusiasm for life grow brighter and brighter until the full light of day. If it helps, start small by setting aside some time before bed to meditate. Then add more time each week. How much time can you start with today?

3. *Sharing the King's Word of Grace*: We saw in Luke 4:18–21 that Christ's gracious words are highlighted in the message of salvation. We can represent our King by sharing His gracious words of salvation with others. Have you ever thought of the gospel in this way? Who can you speak gracious words to this week by sharing the gospel or good news of the kingdom?

4. *Dipping Arrows of Truth in Love*: Psalm 45:4–5 describes the Day when Jesus will return to conquer His enemies by shooting sharp arrows in their heart. However, before that Day, in John 16:7–8 Jesus tells us that the Holy Spirit has come to convict the world concerning sin and righteousness and judgment. The Holy Spirit convicts our hearts of sin through the Word of God (Heb. 4:12). And when the Holy Spirit convicts us of sin, it is like an arrow in the heart that leads us to repent and brings us into glad submission to Jesus.[11] Is the King calling you to represent Him by speaking truth in love (Eph. 4:15; see also Col. 3:16)? How does Christ's love for truth and righteousness give you courage to represent Him?

5. *Getting Involved in Justice Ministries*: Our King loves righteousness and hates wickedness. Therefore, when He returns, He will bring justice to the world (Amos 5:15). The King calls us to represent Him in this age by being part of the mission of setting the oppressed free. Perhaps you have never thought much about this and wonder where to even begin. Might I suggest looking into International Justice Mission? I am a prayer partner of their ministry.

One of my favorite toys that we buy for my daughter are little miniature dolls from different countries. One night I told Jade to select one of the dolls as a representative of the people of that country so we could pray over them. She selected the doll from Thailand. Without going into too much detail, I shared with Jade that some little girls in Thailand are forced into slavery. We prayed together. And in the morning I received an email from International Justice Mission that fourteen girls had been delivered from sex trafficking in Thailand! It was so thrilling to celebrate God's justice with Jade and to take that kingdom adventure together. Begin praying about how to get involved in justice ministries and perhaps talk to your missions team in your local church.

CHAPTER 6

A QUEEN IS BORN

Put first things first and we get second things thrown in: put second things first and we lose both first and second things.

—C. S. Lewis

Do you believe in happy endings?

Perhaps you have been disappointed so many times in this fallen world that you've become cynical and have begun to believe there is no such thing. You roll your eyes and mock those who believe in ideals. Or you're skeptical when people are enthusiastic about life.

Or perhaps you do believe in the happy ending of heaven, but to be honest, you do not live like a woman who will one day receive the staggering inheritance we're discussing throughout this book. Though you have put your faith in Jesus Christ, you have not set your mind on the glories to come. You've become short-sighted.

In *Orthodoxy*, G. K. Chesterton defends Christianity by sharing his personal story of coming to the truth. He uses irony in a masterful way. Fairy tales are for children, people say. But then people grow up and discover truth through a scientific, rational worldview—not so in Chesterton's experience. His journey of coming to the truth was the opposite. He was introduced to some fragments of truth as a child through fairy tales that capture a more accurate view of the world, which has been lost by fallen modern thinkers. One of those elements is that even though something has gone terribly wrong in the world, fairy tales still hold out the possiblity for a happily ever after ending. And Christianity says a happy ending is, in fact, true!

In Psalm 45 we are given a preview of the happy ending God has designed for His people. The most glorious feature of the happy ending is that the Man we have been searching for all our lives really does exist, and He invites us to leave behind our disenchanted lives and to be united with Him. I am eager to walk through the remaining verses in Psalm 45 to show you another thrilling reality; namely, that you, as a believer in Jesus Christ, are in the picture!

BELIEVER—YOU ARE IN THE PICTURE!

Psalm 45 is a messianic psalm, one that points forward to Jesus Christ, as verified in Hebrews 1:8–9. Jesus is the King who will return to restore the world and reign with His bride, the church, by His side. In chapter 5, we entered into the psalmist's excitement for the coming King by gazing on His glories. Now I want to stir your heart with one more glorious feature of the King; namely, He will take for Himself a bride, which is the church:

> Daughters of kings are among your ladies of honor; at your right hand stands the queen in gold of Ophir.
> Hear, O daughter, and consider, and incline your ear: forget your people and your father's house, and the king will

desire your beauty. Since he is your lord, bow to him. The people of Tyre will seek your favor with gifts, the richest of the people.

All glorious is the princess in her chamber, with robes interwoven with gold. In many-colored robes she is led to the king, with her virgin companions following behind her. With joy and gladness they are led along as they enter the palace of the king.

In place of your fathers shall be your sons; you will make them princes in all the earth. I will cause your name to be remembered in all generations; therefore nations will praise you forever and ever. (Ps. 45:9–17)

Let me explain why I refer to Jesus' decision to take a bride as another glorious feature of the King. My husband likes to watch action movies with heroic victories. Of course, these movies often involve fight scenes and the bloodshed necessary to bring about a just resolution. I enjoy some of these films with him. However, I do not usually feel satisfied at the end of a heroic film if the warrior walks off like a lone ranger. There needs to be some romance in the movie to complete it!

Am I just a romantic? Perhaps. But I think there is a more fundamental answer. God is a deeply relational being, and He made us in His relational image. We are *made* for an intimate relationship with God. As a result, it is attractive to us when we see a man who is more than just a warrior. It is attractive to see a warrior who is also a lover!

When Jesus returns, His enemies will be struck with terror by the "awesome deeds" that He will exert by His power (v. 4). Believers will marvel at Christ's conquering power to bring about justice and to reform the universe (2 Thess. 1:9–10). However, the King's conquest of the world is not where the universal narrative ends. Jesus will not walk off the world scene as a lone ranger. He will take for Himself a bride, the church for which He died. And we will see that Jesus is not only a mighty and victorious Warrior, but that He is also a Lover!

I'm not sure how you feel about seeing Jesus in this way. It is hard to conceive of a God who is far greater than we are and who does not need us, but wants to be in an intimate relationship with us and actually *desires the beauty of His people* (Ps. 45:10–11). Maybe in some sense it does seem too wonderful and good to be true.

Yet there is no way of getting around it. As soon as we pick up the Bible, we find God using the most intimate language He has given to us on earth to describe His love and relationship with His people: the language of marriage. In Genesis 2:24 God institutes marriage. Then in Ephesians 5 we are told that God designed marriage to give us a foretaste of the relationship that would one day exist between Jesus Christ and those who trust in Him—the church:

> "A man shall leave his father and mother and hold fast to his wife, and the two shall become one flesh." This mystery is profound, and I am saying that it refers to Christ and the church. (Eph. 5:31–32)

Did you catch that? God designed marriage between a man and a woman in this life to give us an idea, metaphor, or foretaste of the far greater intimacy, joy, and (nonsexual) ecstasy believers will experience with Jesus—a relationship that begins in this life and will be experienced fully in the Age to Come. This is really a stunning truth that we should not pass by too quickly. So let's linger over it a bit longer.

We yearn to experience deep connection with the most excellent of men. Single women may be preoccupied with the thought that today may be the day they will meet a man at the gym, a restaurant, or wherever they go. And for some, each venture back home without that meeting can leave them feeling disappointed. And even married women may struggle with fantasies and temptations to be with someone better than their husband. But Psalm 45 reveals that we do not have to remain in these disenchanted cycles.

God did not design marriage between a man and a woman to be the end all. In fact, Jesus tells us in the Age to Come that there will not be marriage or giving of marriage between a man and a woman (Matt. 22:30). A day is coming when this earthly metaphor will no longer be necessary. Earthly marriage will be replaced

The One we are ultimately longing for is Christ.

with the far greater reality to which it has always pointed! Believers are destined for an intimate and pleasurable relationship with Jesus Christ in the Age to Come. As John Piper has said, "The pleasures of marriage, ten-to-the-millionth power, will be there."[3]

When we begin to meditate on the biblical pictures of the most excellent of men returning soon for His church, we will be able to replace despairing thoughts and sinful fantasies with powerful truths. And instead, we will grow in our devotion to Jesus. On our lonely days, we will recognize that we are experiencing the effects of waiting—waiting to be in the physical presence of Jesus, who is always with us, yet who we are longing to see face to face. And when we are tempted to linger over immoral thoughts, we will be able to pull our minds back by reminding ourselves that the One we are ultimately longing for is Christ. We strive-- as the people of God—to wait with faithfulness and holiness for our coming Groom.

CHRIST'S LOVE FOR HIS BRIDE

The Gospels tell the story of the King who came to seek His bride and die for her in order to bring her back to Himself. And Psalm 45 points to the day when the King will return a second time to marry His bride. The wedding concept in this messianic psalm is filled out in more detail in Revelation 19:6–9, where the church is specifically identified as the bride of Christ.[2] Until that day of Christ's return, the apostle Paul describes the church as being betrothed or engaged to Jesus. "I feel a divine jealousy for you, since I betrothed you to one husband, to present you as a pure virgin to Christ" (2 Cor. 11:2). And during this time of engagement, Jesus is sanctifying or beautifying His bride through the work of the Holy Spirit until He returns:

> Husbands, love your wives, as Christ loved the church and gave himself up for her, that he might sanctify her . . . so that he might present the church to himself in splendor, without spot or wrinkle or any such thing, that she might be holy and without blemish. (Eph. 5:25–27)

Christ's love for His bride is beautiful. He has set her free from the dominating power of sin. And He calls her to come out of her dungeons to dine with Him. His process of beautifying His bride is one of intimacy and love. As she beholds the beauty of His character and ways through Scripture, the Holy Spirit begins conforming her life to the One she loves (2 Cor. 3:18).

Jesus conforms our lives to His in an intimate and beautiful way.

And this is not a foreign concept to us. Think with me about what it is like when a woman is swept up in love with a man. It all begins when her eyes are opened to him as altogether attractive, and she becomes enthralled with his ways.

It is not long before she begins thinking about him throughout the day because it brings her pleasure to picture his handsome features in her mind. In fact, there are times when she cannot get him out of her mind because her desires keep interrupting her thoughts, putting him in the forefront! It is only a matter of time before thinking about the man leads the woman to want to be with him, to communicate her love to him, and to experience life with him.

In a similar way, as we behold Christ's glory, we will start conforming to the One we love in personal holiness. "And we all, with unveiled face, beholding the glory of the Lord, are being transformed into the same image from one degree of glory to another. For this comes from the Lord who is the Spirit" (2 Cor. 3:18).[4]

GETTING READY!

Christ's church—His bride—is called to delight in her love for Him and actively pursue a life that conforms to His by the power of the Holy Spirit at work within her. By doing this, she will honor Him and, as we will see momentarily, He will delight in her beauty! In fact, when Revelation 19 gives us a preview of the future marriage supper of the Lamb, we are told that the bride *has made herself ready*:

> "Hallelujah! For the Lord our God the Almighty reigns. Let us rejoice and exult and give him the glory, for the marriage of the Lamb has come, and his Bride has made herself ready; it was granted her to clothe herself with fine linen, bright and pure"—for the fine linen is the righteous deeds of the saints. (vv. 6–8)

It is important to remember that until our Bridegroom returns, we are still living in a fallen world where Satan seeks to lead us astray from our sincere and pure devotion to Christ as he did with Eve. "But I am afraid that as the serpent deceived Eve by his cunning, your thoughts will be led astray from a sincere and pure devotion to Christ" (2 Cor. 11:3).

God teaches us to set our minds on the things above (Col. 3:2). And Satan tempts us to set our minds on images and pictures of idolatrous loves in this fallen world. There really is no middle road. We *cannot* allow forbidden images to linger in our minds, holding us in the sway of seduction, because it will not be long before we are led astray by our desires. We will find ourselves drunk with lust and will no longer tremble with fear when we consider the end of that matter as described in James 1:14–15: "But each person is tempted when he is lured and enticed by his own desire. *Then desire when it has conceived gives birth to sin, and sin when it is fully grown brings forth death.*"

Pick your poison—seduction comes through many forms of idolatry. Some of us are tempted to throw off God's good limits and set sail into godless romantic adventures once again. Others are tempted to build their own kingdoms and crowns—we can do this even in the church! And others can be tempted to store up treasures and build their own castles in this perishing world instead of using their resources for the kingdom of God. But in keeping with Paul's point above, Satan's aim is to lead us away from our sincere and pure devotion to Christ.

We need to know our self and our weakness because Satan certainly does! And until we reach eternity's shores, temptations will come in and out of our lives enticing us to return to our sinful ways of seeking kings, crowns, kingdoms, and castles apart from God.

- We need to have an accountability partner—someone we can go to for help when Satan's seductive temptations are presented before our eyes (Heb. 10:24–25).
- We need to put on the full armor of God, which includes standing on His Word and praying (Eph. 6:10–20).
- We need to shut off the avenues of temptation that are attempting to set our deceitful desires aflame.
- We need to spend time detoxing by replacing the images of the forbidden thoughts in our minds and begin meditating on biblical pictures of the most excellent of men. And as we do this, the images of our Bridegroom will pull our minds back from the temptation to go slumming in our sin by chasing after other lovers.

Fortunately, our Groom is a jealous God (Ex. 20:5; Hos. 2:5–7). I don't know how long you have been walking with Christ, but I have been with Him long enough to know His jealous love quite well. He is faithful to fight for my affections by thwarting my sinful steps before they turn into full-blown ventures that lead me far away from Him. I am so thankful our Groom cares enough to bring whatever is necessary upon us to sober us up when we become drunk with deceitful desires that tempt us to sail away from the One we love.

INSTRUCTIONS FOR THE BRIDE-QUEEN

Jesus has taken for Himself a bride, His church. He gave His life to save her, cleanse her, and He will fight for her until He returns to bring her into a face-to-face relationship with Him. In Psalm 45:10–11 the bride is given three instructions: (1) hear, consider, and incline your ear, (2) forget your people and your father's house, and (3) bow to the King.

I still marvel at the sacred night when the King came for me. He drew me to a church where I heard and considered the gospel for the first time. The gospel message perfectly diagnosed my soul. As St. Augustine said, "O God, you made us for yourself and our heart remains restless until it finds rest in you."[5] I am made for God. And so are you. Yet we have all exchanged God for the lesser things He has made in creation. But that night I learned that Jesus Christ died for my sin. I heard the good news that if I repented of my sin and submitted to Jesus Christ as Lord, then I would be reconciled back to Him.

Repentance sounded like a divorce to me. And certainly the Bible teaches that it is. Repentance is divorcing, separating, or turning away from our fallen, sinful loyalties in this world so we can turn to Jesus in complete surrender as our Lord and be united with Him as our highest and most devoted Love. Repentance is recognizing that our fallen desires have deceived us and that we were foolish to think we would be happy with kings, kingdoms, castles, or crowns apart from God. Repentance is hearing the good news that our Husband wants us back; therefore, we forget what lies behind—even our dearest loyalties, if they com-

Have you transferred your loyalty back to the One for whom you are made? Have you bowed to the King of kings? If not, why not?

pete with our loyalty to Christ—so that we can take hold of Him.

Unsure of what exactly would become of my life, I *bowed* in submission and adoration to the King, who that night became *my* King. And I went home to end my relationship with a fallen man in order to take hold of the most excellent of men. I had no clue that night how good Jesus would be to me. I just knew that I had found the One my heart has always longed for. And that was all I needed. Like a woman willing to give up everything to take hold of the One she loves, I went home without a care in the world. I had found my true King.

What about you? Have you transferred your loyalty back to the One for whom you are made? Have you bowed to the King of kings? If not, why not? Are you afraid? I can relate. There was a time of wrestling in my soul prior to my submission to Christ. I remember thinking, *What if I am the one person this does not work out for? What if I give up an unhealthy relationship, hungover mornings, and the like?*

It seems absurd to me now that I wrestled over surrendering such empty ways of life. But at the time I was saying goodbye to things that had been lifelong companions—though certainly not friends. Years later I noticed something stunning in Romans 10:9–13 that may be a word of encouragement to you. These verses teach a person how to be saved; namely, by acknowledging that Jesus is Lord and putting your trust in Him:

> If you confess with your mouth that Jesus is Lord and believe in your heart that God raised him from the dead, you will be saved. For with the heart one believes and is justified, and with the mouth one confesses and is saved. (vv. 9–10)

Now notice something powerful in the next three verses. It is as if God anticipates the questions and hesitations that can flood our hearts in the moment of His call to salvation because He assures us that we will not be the one person this does not work out for:

> For the Scripture says, "Everyone who believes in him will not be put to shame." For there is no distinction between Jew or Greek; for the same Lord is Lord of all, bestowing his riches on all who call on him. For "everyone who calls on the name of the Lord will be saved." (vv. 11–13)

Jesus is the same Lord of all, bestowing riches on all who call on Him. I was not the one person this did not work out for, and you will not be either. Looking back, I realize that my moment of wrestling was completely absurd, like a woman who is afraid to drop a snake in order to take hold of a good King and His glorious kingdom. Jesus is real, and He will be faithful to you!

THE GOODNESS OF THE KING TO HIS BRIDE

It is hard to fathom the love Jesus has for His bride and all the extravagant things He has done for her. When a man and a woman marry, they hold everything in common—what is mine is yours and what is yours is mine. One benefit Jesus graciously gives His bride through her union with Him is that He takes away her sin as a Bridegroom takes on his bride's debt. Then He clothes His bride with His righteousness and allows her to partake in His riches.[6]

In keeping with the metaphor of marriage, we see that all the blessings bestowed on believers are described in the New Testament as coming from our union with Jesus Christ: "Blessed be the God and Father of our Lord Jesus Christ, who has blessed us *in Christ* with every spiritual blessing in the heavenly places" (Eph. 1:3).

And our union with Christ results in an ironic twist of fate! When we seek happiness apart from the King, we lose everything. But when God empowers us through the gospel to return to Him, we discover that He truly is all we long for and need. And when we spend time with the King through His Word, He begins to tell us about secondary blessings that He will lavish upon His bride—blessings that begin now and will be experienced in their fullness in the Age to Come. As C. S. Lewis once said, "Put first things first and we get second things thrown in: put second things first and we lose both first and second things."[7] So let's take a closer look at some of the secondary blessings the King will bestow on His queen.

The King will desire His Bride-queen's beauty

Hear, O daughter, and consider, and incline your ear: forget your people and your father's house, and the king will desire your beauty. (Ps. 45:10–11)

I love how Psalm 45 begins by showing us the excellence of the King. And just when we are caught up in awe of Him, something stunning happens. He looks at His church and says, "I desire you." It is one thing to admire and love someone's charming features from a distance. But relational love, intimacy, and joy erupt between two people when the one you desire says he desires you as well! There is a side of me that wants to scratch my head, check the front cover of the book I am reading, and say, "Is this really the Bible?" But again, there is no way around it. God says things like this all throughout Scripture. Let me present you with one more example so you can see that I am not overreaching here:

> You shall be a crown of beauty in the hand of the LORD, and a royal diadem in the hand of your God. You shall no more be termed Forsaken, and your land shall no more be termed Desolate, but you shall be called My Delight Is in Her, and your land Married; for the LORD delights in you, and your land shall be married. . . . as the bridegroom rejoices over the bride, so shall your God rejoice over you. (Isa. 62:3–5)

The Bride-queen will be all-glorious and clothed in fine garments

> All glorious is the princess in her chamber, with robes interwoven with gold. In many-colored robes she is led to the king. (Ps. 45:13–14a)

When we see Jesus face to face we will be made morally perfect (1 John 3:2). I cannot even imagine the day when our sin is completely removed from our souls. The battle for our affections will come to a complete end, and we will be bound together in faithful love to our King forever. We will be dressed in glorious garments—and all the women said, "Amen!" And we will be made all-glorious by the grace of our King—it is hard to fathom the bridal dignity the King will lavish upon us.

The Bride-queen will be led forth with joy and gladness as they enter the palace of the king.

> With joy and gladness they are led along as they enter the palace of the king. (Ps. 45:15)

Adam and Eve were exiled from Eden due to sin. But there is a day coming when we will enter into the palace of the King and experience a kind of intimacy and joy with Him that, as we have seen throughout this chapter, is best understood now through the metaphor of marriage. We will be filled with the fullness of joy in the presence of our King forever (Ps. 16:11) and enter into glorious dwelling places with Him.

God will rule the world through His Bride-queen

> In place of your fathers shall be your sons; you will make them princes in all the earth. I will cause your name to be remembered in all generations; therefore nations will praise you forever and ever. (Ps. 45:16–17)

God created Adam and Eve to rule or govern the earth in subjection to Him. But despite the fall, God did not change His plan for the world. Instead, He is re-creating the world. And when He does, He will rule the world through His church. "We are destined to share in the governing of the universe with divine-like authority."[8] And this of course will be the fulfillment of God's promise to Abraham and David.

A day is coming when the faith of believers in Jesus Christ will give way to sight. Psalm 45 beckons us to enter into this powerful picture to taste and see what it will be like when we are fully united to our King in His kingdom with crowns and palaces restored by His grace. Despite the fact that things have gone terribly wrong in the world, Christianity affirms that there is a happily ever after ending for those who bow to Jesus Christ, which is far greater than any destiny we could imagine on our own. And His extravagant love for His bride will cause us to live in awe of Him. "I will cause your name to be remembered in all generations; therefore nations will praise you forever and ever" (Ps. 45:17).

ENTHUSIASM FOR THE GOSPEL AND EVANGELISM

Psalm 45 will lead us to marvel at the gospel and motivate us to tell others the good news. In John 3, Jesus teaches that we must be spiritually born again. As we have said, God causes a woman to be spiritually born again when she hears the gospel and believes by repenting of her sin and submitting to Jesus Christ. And when we consider John 3 in view of the fullness of our salvation seen through Psalm 45, we can say that when a woman believes in Jesus Christ, a queen is born! She has not yet stepped into the fullness of her salvation, but she will one day rule with Christ in submission to Him.

This is humbling and awakens great enthusiasm in me for the gospel and evangelism! Consider this with me: when the Holy

Spirit stirs in your heart to knock on the door of a sinful woman, it is because the King is seeking His bride. When a woman opens the door looking worn down by her wayward life, you share the gospel with her, and faith rises up in her heart resulting in new spiritual birth—do you know what just took place? She is united to Jesus Christ, the King of kings, and will one day rule and reign with Him. Astonishing! Like John the Baptist, we are invited to participate in the great joy of leading people to Jesus Christ, the Bridegroom, and watch Him lavish His love upon His bride (John 3:29).

MOVING FROM GUTTERS
OF SIN TO GLORY WITH HIM

1. Your decision to submit to Jesus Christ is the most important decision of your life. Meditate on living in the joy of Christ's presence and enjoying pleasures at His right hand forevermore through Psalm 45. Then, meditate on Matthew 7:23, where Jesus says to those who refuse to submit to Him, "I never knew you; depart from me, you workers of lawlessness." Can you imagine how terrifying it will be when a person is shut out of the presence of Christ and the pleasures in His kingdom forever? Does this truth move you to submit to Jesus Christ today? If you have already surrendered your life to Jesus, then write down some names of unbelievers you can share this message with and begin praying for their salvation.

2. Please read 2 Corinthians 11:2. Is there any area of your life where you can see that Satan is attempting to lead you astray from your pure devotion to Christ? If yes, make the decision now to rule over your sin instead of allowing it to rule over you (Rom. 6:12–14; Gen. 4:7; Ps. 119:133). Fight your sin by considering how God's good laws and limits make your life richer in Christ (chapter 3). Meditate by picturing, pondering, and praying over: (1) the extravagant love of Christ for you as seen here in Psalm 45, and (2) the Judgment Seat of Christ as seen in 2 Corinthians 5:9–10. Contact a friend to pray for you and hold you accountable.

3. A single woman once shared with me that she feels ashamed for being single. The root of her shame was feeling undesired.

Some married women feel undesired by their husbands as well. Meditate on the love of Christ for His bride through Psalm 45 each day this week. Write down new insights on how the bridal dignity of the church begins to remove illegitimate shame you may feel. At the end of the week, record how your bridal dignity and joy in Christ can empower you to serve your husband and others.

4. Make time this week to meditate on Revelation 19:6–9. How does this powerful picture motivate you to make yourself ready for our coming King-Groom? Read 2 Peter 1:3–11. How can you begin growing out of cycles of sin by participating in this glorious cycle of holiness, moving from gutters to glory?

5. Please read Ephesians 5:22–23. If you are married, how has this chapter inspired you to make changes in your marriage to reflect Christ and the church?

CHAPTER 7

A DOWN-TO-EARTH WOMAN

It takes courage to grow up and become who you really are.
—E. E. Cummings

Christianity creates women who are enthusiastic about our King and life with Him in the Age to Come. But as we grow in our understanding of what Paul calls the "whole counsel of God" (Acts 20:27), we will also become a *down-to-earth* woman as well. In other words, as we understand the whole biblical story about life and salvation, we will have a robust understanding of both the Age to Come and what Galatians 1:4 calls the "present evil age," in which we still live.

Learning and applying the whole counsel of God to our lives is powerful (James 1:22–23). The result is that we will become equipped to lead our children, family, friends, and neighbors into the wonder of Christianity, while also helping them understand God's purposes for us as we journey through this fallen world to the city of God.

I remember attending a Christian conference years ago, tucked away in a rustic mountain range. The landscape was covered with brush, and we stayed in wood cabins connected by dirt roads. One afternoon a woman who was part of the prosperity gospel movement walked into the room wearing a fur coat, high heels, and gaudy jewelry. Trailing behind her was a driver carrying her bags. She swept into the room with airs while everyone else was working busily in our workshops. The woman seemed out of touch with reality as if living an illusion or pretense—in a world of her own. While the world is on fire around us and there is much gospel work to be done, she seemed to be sitting in her castle inappropriately ahead of her time. Of course, I could not know the woman's heart. She may have been a wonderful wife and mother, a loyal friend, and served God in different ways. But on that particular day, she did not look prepared to wash anyone's feet or bear anyone else's burdens, but was rather looking to be served by others (Mark 10:45).

DOWN-TO-EARTH PROMISES

When we look at Jesus in the Gospels, we see a Man who is passionate about the Age to Come. And yet He does not overlook the realities of evil, sin, and suffering in this fallen world. We see Jesus' lofty promises and down-to-earth perspective woven together in Matthew 19–20. Jesus tells His disciples they will sit on thrones with Him in the new world (19:28). And yet, when the mother of James and John asks Jesus to give her sons seats of honor in His kingdom, Jesus says they will first share in His suffering (20:23).

When we apply Christ's teachings to our lives and imitate His example, we will grow in a high and holy enthusiasm for our new life with Him, which begins now and will be consummated in the Age to Come. But we will also learn how to be effective in the gospel ministry as we humbly serve people and help them navigate through the sin and suffering in this fallen world.

> But Jesus called them to him and said, "You know that the rulers of the Gentiles lord it over them, and their great ones exercise authority over them. It shall not be so among you. But whoever would be great among you must be your servant, and whoever would be first among you must be your slave, even as the Son of Man came not to be served but to serve, and to give his life as a ransom for many." (Matt. 20:25–28)

INAPPROPRIATELY AHEAD OF TIME

In Psalm 45 the Holy Spirit stirs our enthusiasm for the coming King and the destiny of believers. But sometimes people get confused about *timing*. Some have fallen into error by thinking and living as though Christ's kingdom has been fully realized in this age. Some people may try to claim the full measure of blessings in this age that will not actually be available until the Age to Come. They're out of step with what God is doing in this present age and become ineffective for gospel ministry.

In Paul's first letter to the Corinthians, we learn that the church was struggling with pride. They were beginning to overlook the reality of sin and struggle in this age and were living with a sense of premature triumphalism. Furthermore, they had a self-centered enthusiasm concerning wisdom, spiritual gifts, and the power of the Holy Spirit.[1]

In 1 Corinthians 4:8–17 Paul uses irony and a powerful metaphor to bring the church down to earth:

> Already you have all you want! Already you have become rich! Without us you have become kings! And would that you did reign, so that we might share the rule with you! For I think that God has exhibited us apostles as last of all, like men sentenced to death, because we have become a spectacle to the world, to angels, and to men. We are fools for Christ's sake, but you are wise in Christ. We are weak, but you are strong. You are held in honor, but we in disrepute. To the present hour we hunger and thirst, we are poorly dressed and buffeted and homeless, and we labor, working with our own hands. When reviled, we bless; when persecuted, we endure; when slandered, we entreat. We have become, and are still, like the scum of the world, the refuse of all things.
>
> I do not write these things to make you ashamed, but to admonish you as my beloved children. For though you have countless guides in Christ, you do not have many fathers. For I became your father in Christ Jesus through the gospel. I urge you, then, be imitators of me. That is why I sent you Timothy, my beloved and faithful child in the Lord, to remind you of my ways in Christ, as I teach them everywhere in every church.

The Corinthians were living as though Christ's kingdom had already been fully realized. They were living like they were full, rich, and reigning now.[2] Mistiming is emphasized when Paul says "already" they have become full and rich (v. 8), but "to the present hour we" (Paul and his companions) hunger and thirst and are poorly dressed (v. 11). Paul corrects the Corinthians using stinging irony. He says you are living as though you have become kings "without us" (the apostles and Paul—their spiritual father) (v. 8). Indeed, Paul says, it would be wonderful if you were reigning now because then we would be ruling too!

Paul continues to bring the church down to earth by following his irony with a metaphor of gladiators ("a spectacle," v. 9) in an arena. He uses this image to draw a contrast between the apostles, who are like gladiators, sharing in the sufferings of Christ versus the Corinthians, who were living as spectators with comfortable seats on their thrones.[3]

Gladiators were despised. They were viewed as the scum of the world. And entering into the arena as a spectacle to fight beast or man was a death sentence because the two participants would fight to the death of one of them. Paul's point is powerful. In this present age, believers are called to participate in a cosmic spiritual battle. We are to get into the arena of gospel ministry, which will inevitably require us to share in the sufferings of Christ. To live as though we are rich and reigning now would be inappropriately ahead of our time.

Paul begins this section by teaching us how to view ourselves in this age. He says that here on earth we should think of ourselves as "servants" and "stewards of the mysteries of God," and adds that "it is required of stewards that they be found faithful" (1 Cor. 4:1–2).

A steward is given the responsibility of overseeing or managing an owner's estate; in other words, we have been made stewards of God's kingdom. Stewards must be found faithful or trustworthy to the desires and instructions of the owner. Paul goes on to say that when Jesus returns, He will assess at the proper time how faithful we have been (vv. 3–5).

We will talk more about the judgment seat of Christ in chapter 10. But for now I would like to make the point that we're still on the clock; it is not time to sit down on the job. We cannot enjoy our reward until we are done with the work God has given us to do. So let's learn how to become more faithful in our stewardship of the kingdom by taking a closer look at God's plans for the two ages.

IN BOTH TIMES

The New Testament reveals that there are two ages—this present age and the Age to Come. We see this in various passages, but one example is Matthew 12:32, where Jesus says, "Whoever speaks against the Holy Spirit will not be forgiven, either in *this age* or the *age to come*." This age began when God created the world and will extend to the return of Jesus Christ.

In Galatians 1:4, Paul calls this age "the present evil age." Paul is not describing this age as evil in itself, but when humanity fell from glory in Genesis 3, it became "the age of human existence in weakness and mortality, of evil, sin, and death."[4] When Jesus rose from the dead and ascended to heaven, He was enthroned. Jesus is the King now. But He must also become King in the sense that when He returns He will remove sin, evil, and death from the world and manifest His glorious kingdom throughout the world (1 Cor. 15:24–28). When Jesus returns, this age will come to a close and the Age to Come will be inaugurated. *At that time*, we will enter into the full measure of blessing under God's rule as His beloved children (Luke 20:34–36, Matt. 19:28).[5]

In the Age to Come we will see the realization of all God's promises—we will experience the fulfillment of everything we have desired and anticipated. To help you understand what we mean by the word "realization," let's use the word in a way that someone might use it in this life.

Someone might say, "I am grateful that my mom lived long enough to see the realization of what she hoped for. She has prayed for years that her children would come to know the Lord, and now they have." Now, when we use "realization" to describe the destiny of believers, we are saying that in the Age to Come we will see the realization of *everything* God has promised, all that we have desired and anticipated.

Jesus is doing extraordinary kingdom works even through the weakness, sin, and suffering in this present age!

So far, so good; everything seems clear-cut. But something unique happened when Jesus came two thousand years ago; namely, the kingdom of God interrupted this present evil age through the Person and work of Jesus Christ. For this reason, Jesus talks about the kingdom of God as both a present and future reality. When asked by the Pharisees when this kingdom would come, Jesus replied, "the kingdom of God is in the midst of you" (Luke 17:20–21). The kingdom of God is a present reality; it is here, in your midst. But Jesus also teaches that the kingdom of God will come in the future:

As they heard these things, he proceeded to tell a parable, because he was near to Jerusalem, and because they supposed that the kingdom of God was to appear immediately. He said therefore, "A nobleman went into a far country to receive for himself a kingdom and then return." (Luke 19:11–12)

And so we see that the coming of the kingdom of God is a present event and a future event as well. How do we put this together? The kingdom of God has come, but we eagerly await the final consummation. The kingdom of God comes into the lives of people who obey the gospel by repenting of their sin and submitting to Jesus Christ in this age. Believers are rescued from the dominion of darkness and brought into the kingdom of God's beloved Son (Col. 1:13). But, we will not step into the *fullness* of God's promises until Jesus returns to remove everything in opposition to Himself and manifest His glorious kingdom to the ends of the earth.

As a result, believers are said to live in both ages. We still live in the old age. Yet, the powers of the new age have begun in our lives. Thus we begin to experience some of the blessings and power of living under God's good reign now, but we will not enter into the fullness of these blessings until the consummation of the kingdom.[6] We will see momentarily what Jesus is doing in the time between His first and second coming. But for now I want to note that Jesus is doing extraordinary kingdom works even through the weakness, sin, and suffering in this present age!

Let me give you an example. In the Age to Come all believers will be healed from sickness, and God will clothe us with immortality (Luke 20:36). This is really a stunning reality—we will never experience death again! But death has not been removed from reality in this present age. We will all die once (except those who are alive when Christ returns).

Nevertheless, we do see the powers of the new age come upon people in this age when Jesus heals people as recorded in the Gospels (Mark 5:34; 10:52). And these moments are truly thrilling because they give us previews of the Age to Come. Thus, we should pray for healing when we are sick (James 5:13–15). But we must also recognize that Jesus did not heal everyone while He was on earth, and He does not heal everyone in this age.[7] Yet God still shows Himself glorious in the midst of sin and suffering because He uses it to bring about the salvation of many.

I have a friend whose son had a birth defect. When she was pregnant the doctors told her that her son would die shortly after he was born. She and her family prayed for healing. But after she held her babe for thirty-one minutes, smelling his newborn scent, and stroking his delicate fingers, his soul returned to his Maker. She was heartbroken. As a mother, I weep every time I tell this story; yep, I am weeping right now as I type. I cannot wait until the Age to Come when there will be no more death, no more goodbyes, no more separation sorrow from the ones we love. But consider what God has done and continues to do through this sickness and death.

In time, my friend became a leader in a ministry that makes hope boxes for women who are walking through infant loss. She raises funds to create beautiful boxes that contain Bibles, books, and other materials that lead grieving women to find hope in Christ. In each box is a handwritten note from another mother who has also walked through infant loss and found hope in Christ. My friend takes these boxes to the hospital where her son died, and the hospital gives them to other women who experience the loss of an infant. This is a beautiful picture of Christlike humility that considers others.

Can you imagine? When a babe is removed from a woman's arms, a box is put into her hands, which may lead her to find salvation and hope in Jesus Christ. If my friend had not walked through this suffering, she would not have been able to comfort others with the comfort she had received from Christ (2 Cor. 1:4). Even to this day, my friend sows the seeds of the gospel with tears.

Living in both ages requires wisdom and skill.

But she reaps high, high measures of joy when she meets women who have been saved and encouraged through her son's thirty-one minutes of life!

Living in both ages requires wisdom and skill. We do not want to be inappropriately ahead of our time by demanding God do things in this age that He has not promised to do until the Age to Come. Yet we want to earnestly seek God for as much kingdom power as He is pleased to grant us in order to advance the gospel and His kingdom into the lives of others![8]

And, like the apostle Paul and my friend described above, we should be ready to recognize how God uses the sin and sufferings in this present age to accomplish glorious kingdom works. So let's take a closer look at this present age and what Jesus is doing in our midst so we can learn how to get in the game as down-to-earth women.

WORLDWIDE OPPOSITION TO THE KING

I would like to invite you to pause and read Psalm 2, another messianic psalm. Acts 4:25 tells us that the Holy Spirit spoke through the mouth of David in Psalm 2. In this psalm David is looking forward to his future descendant who will sit on his throne and rule forever. This psalm is thrilling because it is about the unstoppable, victorious King—the One who will fulfill God's promise in Genesis 3:15 that an offspring of Eve will crush the head of the serpent and the One who will fulfill the promise given to Abraham and David.

But in Psalm 2, David realizes something else about the coming King, which is important for us to understand as well: there will be worldwide opposition to Him. The nations will rage against the Lord and His anointed King. They will set themselves against Him saying, "Let us burst their bonds apart and cast away their cords from us" (Ps. 2:3). They have cast off God as their Ruler, and they have cast off His "bonds and cords," that is, His morally good ways.

We still see people and nations raging against the Lord and casting off His morally good ways today. Turn on the news, and you will see what Charles Colson called a "militant secularism."[9] Unbelievers pride themselves on being "independent thinkers." In other words, they pride themselves on being independent of God. And even those who are more drawn to mysticism than materialism often prefer to identify themselves as "spiritual" rather than "religious." Colson observes that the word "religion" comes from the Latin word *ligare*, "to bind." And we can hear the sound of "obedience" in the word "religion," which is distasteful to those who have thrown off God's rule and moral law.[10]

People and nations are still raging against God's anointed King and those who represent Him by teaching His ways. Consider the uproar we hear when a follower of Christ says abortion and homosexual practice are morally wrong.

But in Psalm 2:4 we are told that "He who sits in the heavens laughs; the Lord holds them in derision." The nations rage against the Lord and His King in vain because God will put His Son on the worldwide throne and no one will overcome His rule. We see the climax of the prophecy given to us in Psalm 2 at the crucifixion of Jesus Christ. The kings and rulers of the earth take their stand against the Lord and His anointed King to such an extent that they kill Him on the cross!

A CROWN OF THORNS

In John 18, we read of Jesus being put on trial. Pilate, the Roman governor, calls Him into a private conversation to see if Jesus is a political threat to Rome. In verse 33 Pilate asks Jesus, "Are you the King of the Jews?" Jesus answers, "My kingdom is not of this world. If my kingdom were of this world, my servants would have been fighting, that I might not be delivered over to the Jews. But my kingdom is not from the world" (v. 36).

In other words, Jesus reveals that His kingdom will not come by rebellion or terrorism. His kingdom is from heaven, and though Jesus does not explain this to Pilate at the time, His kingdom comes into a person's life when she submits to Jesus and is born again by faith in Him (John 3:3). At that point she is delivered from Satan's kingdom into God's kingdom (Col. 1:13).[11]

Jesus did not come to fight a military battle against Rome or other nations. Jesus came to fight a spiritual battle. He came to defeat Satan on the cross and deliver people from sin and Satan's kingdom. This is the saving work Jesus is doing in our midst today and will continue to do until He returns. Then, when the King returns, He will "dash" into pieces the rulers and nations who are in opposition to Him, making the ends of the earth His possession (Ps. 2:8–9).

When Pilate heard "kingdom," he said, "So you are a king?" (John 18:37). And Jesus replied that His kingdom is not like Rome's. Christ's kingdom is a kingdom of truth, and Jesus came into the world to testify to the truth. Pilate responds similarly to the postmodern spirit that reigns in our day: "What is truth?" (v. 38).

After throwing off God's rule and moral law, people have no standard to live by. As a result, they create their own meaning based on what makes them happy and have become like Pilate, a person devoid of truth, justice, conviction, and courage. Though Pilate knew Jesus was innocent, he was motivated by cowardice and the fear of man to hand Jesus over to be flogged:

> Then Pilate took Jesus and flogged him. And the soldiers twisted together a crown of thorns and put it on his head and arrayed him in a purple robe. They came up to him, saying, "Hail, King of the Jews!" and struck him with their hands. Pilate went out again and said to them, "See, I am bringing him out to you that you may know that I find no guilt in him." So Jesus came out, wearing the crown of thorns and the purple robe. Pilate said to them, "Behold the man!" (John 19:1–5)

Consider the suffering that the King of heaven endured in this present evil age. He maintained perfect obedience to God's will and humbly served others to the point of death. Jesus is a perfect model of how we are called to humble ourselves and serve others to represent Christ and lead many sons and daughters back to glory. This entire scene—the crown of thorns, purple robe, and beaten body—was intended to mock Jesus. The Jews wanted to portray Jesus as a wannabe King who had been defeated.[12] And when the Jewish authorities wanted Jesus put to death, Pilate went against his conscience and pronounced judgment on the One who will one day judge the world:

> So when Pilate heard these words, he brought Jesus out and sat down on the judgment seat at a place called The Stone Pavement, and in Aramaic Gabbatha. Now it was the day of Preparation of the Passover. It was about the sixth hour. He said to the Jews, "Behold your King!" They cried out, "Away with him, away with him, crucify him!" Pilate said to them, "Shall I crucify your King?" The chief priests answered, "We have no king but Caesar." So he delivered him over to them to be crucified. (John 19:13–16)

The climax Psalm 2 pointed forward to was the crucifixion of Jesus Christ. The nations and rulers were raging against the Lord and His anointed King. And they threw off their bonds declaring, "We have no King." But just as Psalm 2 announces, God's sovereign plan cannot be thwarted. God used the sin of lawless men to accomplish the extravagant and gracious work of salvation that we have been discussing throughout this book. Yes, feel free to pause and marvel. I suppose if we were having coffee together right now, our overflowing words would come to silence, and we would be looking at each other in awe! Jesus endured a crown of thorns and death on the cross so we could partake in the age of crowns to come.

God is gracious and unstoppable. Satan and sinful people cannot oppose God. Instead of waiting until the end of the age,

Jesus entered into this present evil age to defeat Satan, to deliver people from his dark kingdom, and to transfer them into His kingdom of light. Christ's death on the cross was the decisive victory over Satan. When Jesus died on the cross, He canceled the "record of debt that stood against us with its legal demands" (Col. 2:14). As a result, Satan can no longer legitimately accuse or condemn believers of our sin.

Therefore, when Jesus "set aside" our record of debt, "nailing it to the cross," He "disarmed the rulers and authorities and put them to open shame, by triumphing over them" (Col. 2:14–15). Jesus won the battle against Satan by His death and resurrection. Jesus has been enthroned. And when He returns, Satan will be cast in the lake of fire forever, and *all* things will be subjected to Christ. "He must reign until he has put all his enemies under his feet" (1 Cor. 15:25).

GETTING IN THE GOSPEL ARENA

After Jesus rose from the dead, He appeared to His disciples to make a stunning announcement. All authority and power has been given to Jesus, and He is using His authority in a most gracious way. He is calling people to repent of their rebellion before He returns to manifest His kingdom throughout the world:

> "All authority in heaven and on earth has been given to me. Go therefore and make disciples of all nations, baptizing them in the name of the Father and of the Son and of the Holy Spirit, teaching them to observe all that I have commanded you. And behold, I am with you always, to the end of the age." (Matt. 28:18–20)

It is stunning to consider how Jesus has called us to begin participating in the kingly activity of extending His rule into the lives of others through the gospel ministry!

In the Age to Come, God will create a new world and extend His rule through His bride-queen pictured in Psalm 45. We have not arrived on those shores yet—we are not sitting on thrones in heaven. However, it is stunning to consider how Jesus has called *us* to begin participating in the kingly activity of extending His rule into the lives of others through the gospel ministry! We are to represent our King by leading people to repent of their sins, be baptized, and learn how to live in God's good ways.

SPIRITUAL BATTLES

The gospel ministry also inevitably draws us into the cosmic spiritual battle that is taking place in our midst. Listen to how Jesus describes the gospel ministry to Paul in Acts 26:18. Jesus told Paul He was sending him to open the eyes of people "so that they may turn from darkness to light and from the power of Satan to God, that they may receive forgiveness of sins and a place among those who are sanctified by faith in me." Jesus is delivering people from the dominion of Satan. As a result, we are called to participate to some degree in Jesus' kingly activity of engaging in spiritual warfare as we advance the gospel in people's lives.[13]

I can vividly remember the day I realized there is a spiritual battle going on in our midst. I had recently heard and believed the gospel. The eyes of my heart were opened to see Jesus and reality. I had high affections for my newfound King, yet was young and unlearned in the Scriptures. As a result, I had a lot of passion but not much wisdom. One evening my friend and I had a bold idea to return to the underground club in Houston where we used to carouse before meeting Christ, in order to share the gospel with others.

I will never forget how different everything seemed when we walked in. The doors opened at 2:00 a.m. after the other bars had closed. As a result, everyone who entered was already drunk and out of their mind. And to my surprise, the dark and smoky room that I used to roam about recklessly without fear or care now felt eerie and full of evil. As we walked through the rooms I noticed that people lingering in the shadows—who never seemed to be bothered by my presence before—were looking at me as if I did not belong.

And though I was not educated in the Scriptures enough to fully understand or articulate what was happening at the time, I felt humbled, realizing that our idea was brash and that perhaps there were realities in life we should be better equipped to face than we were that night. We did not stay

Jesus has "already" won the victory, but we are "not yet" in the Age to Come.

long. And when we awoke in the morning, we learned my car had been broken into and my friend's car had been stolen—something that had never happened to us before or since.

As I grew in my knowledge of Scripture, I began to understand the reality of spiritual warfare. Before hearing and believing the gospel, I was dead in my sins and "following the prince of the power of the air, the spirit that is now at work in the sons of disobedience" (Eph. 2:1–2). For that reason, I blended right in with others who were lingering in the shadows of sin and evil. But when I was spiritually born again, I was delivered from the power and dominion of Satan.

The demonic world knows to whom I and other believers belong. Furthermore, God gives believers the ability to distinguish between spirits. In other words, believers can often recognize the difference between the presence of the Holy Spirit or demonic spirits (1 John 4:1; 1 Cor. 12:10).[14] And looking back, this may have been the first time I was experiencing this new spiritual awareness, as I was recognizing evil in a way I never had before. That was the night I began to realize what the Bible describes as the spiritual battle taking place in our midst and why Paul calls us to "put on the whole armor of God" (see Eph. 6:10–17).

A spiritual war is taking place around us. Thus, we are not called to sit on thrones in this present evil age. Instead, we are called to imitate Jesus and Paul by getting in the arena of gospel ministry to advance the kingdom of God. It is important to remember that Jesus has "already" won the victory, but we are "not yet" in the Age to Come; therefore, we must participate in the spiritual battle. John Piper says it like this:

> The decisive battle has been won against Satan. It was fought in the life, death and resurrection of Jesus. We now live in a tension as Christians for we are delivered from this present evil age and have our citizenship in heaven, but we are not yet perfected and the flesh, the world and Satan are not yet wholly abolished. Therefore we are more than conquerors but we still must fight.[15]

We are required to participate in a cosmic battle. And it will inevitably require us to share in the sufferings of Christ. Because of opposition to the King, there will also, as a result, be opposition to His bride (2 Cor. 1:5).

OPPOSITION TO THE KING'S BRIDE

After Jesus ascended into heaven, He poured out His Holy Spirit on His disciples. The gospel began to spread, and the church began to grow. Jesus was being proclaimed as the long-awaited King, and people from all races and nations were invited to repent of their sin and become citizens of His kingdom (Acts 3:25–26). In Acts 3, Peter and John were preaching the gospel, and many were being saved:

> "Repent therefore, and turn back, that your sins may be blotted out, that times of refreshing may come from the presence of the Lord, and that he may send the Christ appointed for you, Jesus, whom heaven must receive until the time for restoring all the things about which God spoke by the mouth of his holy prophets long ago." (vv. 19–21)

Threatened by the spread of the gospel, the Jewish authorities put Peter and John in jail and asked by whose authority or power and name they were doing these things (Acts 4:7). Filled with the Holy Spirit, Peter answered them by saying they were doing these things in the authority of Jesus—the One who the Jewish authorities crucified but who was raised from the dead—the only One through whom people can be saved (vv. 8–12). The Jewish authorities commanded the disciples not to speak in the name of Jesus any more. But they loved Jesus and wanted to obey Him and be like Him by serving others.

Therefore, notice what happened when the disciples were released. They returned to their Christian companions and shared all that had occurred. And look at how the believers responded! They prayed Psalm 2 to God and concluded with a specific request:

> "Sovereign Lord, who made the heaven and the earth and the sea and everything in them, who through the mouth of our father David, your servant, said by the Holy Spirit, 'Why did the Gentiles rage, and the peoples plot in vain? The kings of the earth set themselves, and the rulers were gathered together, against the Lord and against his Anointed'—for truly in this city there were gathered together against your holy servant Jesus, whom you anointed, both Herod and Pontius Pilate, along with the Gentiles and the peoples of Israel, to do whatever your hand and your plan had predestined to take place. And now, Lord, look upon their threats and grant to your servants to continue to speak your word with all boldness, while you stretch out your hand to heal, and signs and wonders are performed through the name of your holy servant Jesus." And when they had prayed, the place in which they were gathered together was shaken, and they were all filled with the Holy Spirit and continued to speak the word of God with boldness. (Acts 4:24–31)

The nations rage in vain against God and His King. Massive opposition to Jesus rose to the point that they crucified Him on the cross. And as we see in this passage, there will be opposition to us—His bride, the church. But notice with me how down-to-earth the believers are in this passage! They did not deny or downplay the reality of sin and struggle in this present evil age. Instead, they acknowledged the reality that they will share in the opposition and sufferings of Christ.

Therefore, they asked God to strengthen them to stay in the game. They asked for boldness and courage to continue speaking God's Word. We too will experience God in awesome ways when we align our lives with what He is doing in our midst and pray for boldness and courage to join Him. I have begun praying for God to give me thicker skin! And I want to invite you to join me in doing the same.

A MATTER OF TIME

Battles are bloody. They are painful. People even die. Using the words of E. E. Cummings, "It takes courage to grow up and become who you really are." A great deal of strength and courage come from understanding God's plans and purposes in this age and the Age to Come, allowing us to serve our King faithfully.

Be confident that God's sovereign plan *cannot* be thwarted. Jesus defeated Satan at the cross and has been enthroned. And now He is using believers to extend His kingdom into the lives of others through the *end of the age* (Matt. 28:20). And when our King returns, then we will see that those who suffer with Him in this age will sit on thrones and reign with Him at the renewal of all things: "The one who conquers, I will grant him to sit with me on my throne, as I also conquered and sat down with my Father on his throne" (Rev. 3:21; see also 2 Tim. 2:12). Thus, we should not become idle or prideful, thinking we are already rich and reigning. Instead, we must get into the gospel arena!

BECOMING A DOWN-TO-EARTH WOMAN

Let's not make the mistake of mistiming God's promises. Let's learn how to live in this age, as we eagerly anticipate the fullness of God's promises in the Age to Come. By doing so, we will become down-to-earth women who are filled with enthusiasm and hope and are able to help people practically walk through this present evil age to the city of God.

1. What are some sufferings that tempt you to shrink back from obeying God in the gospel ministry? Read Paul's lists of sufferings in 2 Corinthians 4:7–18 and 11:24–33. List how God uses these sufferings to manifest His glory through Paul's life. How can these insights help you endure sufferings for the kingdom as well?

2. Read Philippians 3:18–20. List Paul's description of false teachers. Write down some ways that false teachers differ from the ministry of Jesus and Paul. In 1 Corinthians 4, we see that genuine believers can make the mistake of mistiming. But in Philippians 3, we see that some professing believers are in fact unbelievers using the gospel for selfish gain. One way to help distinguish between genuine believers who are confused on timing and unbelievers using the gospel for selfish gain is how they respond to correction. Let's look at that more closely in the next question.

3. After Paul rebukes the Corinthians for mistiming, he comforts them in a beautiful Christlike way: "I do not write these things to make you ashamed, but to admonish you as my

beloved children. . . . I urge you, then, be imitators of me" (1 Cor. 4:14, 16). There are parallels between Paul and the Corinthians and Jesus' address to the church at Laodicea. Read Revelation 3:14–22 and write down the parallels between Paul's rebuke to the Corinthians and Jesus' rebuke of the Laodiceans. Notice that both are invited to repent of their sin because Jesus and Paul love them. How does this inspire you to repent of mistiming resulting in laziness? How does this equip you to lovingly help other believers who may have fallen into this error as well?

4. Read 2 Timothy 2:12–13. How does this promise motivate you to identify with Christ and endure suffering with Him?

5. Read Jeremiah 1:17–19, 15:20–21; Ezekiel 3:8–9; and Micah 3:8–9. How does it encourage you to know that God's prophets needed strength from God to stand for Him as well? Begin asking God to give you thicker skin!

CHAPTER 8

THE NEW DYNASTY

And if children, then heirs—heirs of God and fellow
heirs with Christ, provided we suffer with him in order
that we may also be glorified with him.
—Romans 8:17

One morning I received a phone call that my father's mother had died. I packed my bags and returned to the land of my roots to honor my grandma's life and mourn with my family. When I arrived at the funeral home, I saw they were running a slide show of pictures streaming above her casket. The portraits were placed in chronological order telling the broad story of her life.

At one point in the narrative, there was a picture of my grandma and grandpa, as young adults, entering into the joy of marriage together. My grandpa and grandma were standing tall and happy in the back with their beautiful children surrounding them.

But then all of a sudden someone was missing from the pictures. My grandpa had died in a farming accident, changing everyone's life in a dramatic way. In the pictures that followed you could see a single mother trying to be strong for her youngest, my uncle, who was only five years old at the time. There were pictures of my father, who was seventeen, working on the farm as he took over the role of providing for the family. And while their story went on, you could see that their lives were never the same.

As tears streamed down my face, I could not help but see the big human story echoed through my family's personal narrative. The picture of my father's family standing strong, beautiful, and happy together reminded me of God's original design for humanity. But in Genesis 3 the good life was shattered by sin and its consequences, including death. And I wept over the thought of what life could have been like for my family had sin and death not entered the world.

Fortunately, I was not grieving without hope (1 Thess. 4:13–14). My tears were also mingled with adoration and gratitude because, in God's providence, all this took place the week I was writing this chapter. As a result, my mind was filled with the stunning truths that God is in the process of building a new family through Jesus Christ. And I could not stop marveling at the fact that when Jesus returns, we will see a new family portrait.

We will see believers restored to the holy, healthy, and happy lives God intended for us.

We will see believers restored to the holy, healthy, and happy lives God intended for us. Sin and selfishness will shatter precious relationships no more. And death will not separate us from the ones we love. The people standing in the new family portrait will be immortal—we will never experience death again. We will be refreshed and invigorated by our genuine love and unity with one another. And we will set off on family ventures in a new world that has the security of home.

Oh, how I groan in anticipation of that day (Rom. 8:23).

And how I long for everyone in my earthly family and yours to become part of the new family God is creating through Jesus Christ! So let's take a closer look at the stunning family God is creating and how we can become part of it.

THE NEW FAMILY

As previously discussed, God made Adam and Eve to be part of His royal family. Humanity bears God's image like a son bears the image of his father. And God gave humanity the privilege and responsibility to rule the world as His representatives. Though humanity rebelled against God and fell from glory, we have seen that God began moving forward in His gracious plan to restore humanity to His good design for us.

God promised Abraham: "In you all the families of the earth shall be blessed" (Gen. 12:3). In Genesis 17 God takes significant steps forward in the creation of a new royal family by making a covenant with Abraham, assuring him that he will become the father of a multitude of nations (v. 4).

God's plan to create a new family through Abraham is filled out with more detail in 2 Samuel 7 when God makes another covenant with David to build a dynasty or royal family through Him. Jesus was the ultimate fulfillment of this promise. He was born from the line of David and will rule on the worldwide throne forever.[1] And now Jesus is in the process of building a royal family who will submit to His rule and reign with Him forever!

Isn't it incredible? When a person believes in Jesus, she becomes a spiritual descendant of Abraham and David. She has become part of the new dynasty.

And if that weren't enough, God gives His people the gift

of the Holy Spirit, who enlightens our minds and our hearts to know that God is our Father: "Because you are his sons, God sent the Spirit of his Son into our hearts, the Spirit who calls out, '*Abba*, Father.' So you are no longer a slave, but God's child; and since you are his child, God has made you also an heir" (Gal. 4:6–7 NIV). For this reason, we see many passages in the New Testament in which family language is used to address believers in Jesus Christ as beloved children of God, brothers, and sisters.

THE FIRSTBORN

I am eager to show you glorious things about our new family. The apostle John shares a revelation that he received from Jesus Christ of what must soon take place, for the time is near. Let me say that again: the Age to Come is close at hand! John begins the letter by greeting the churches using wonderful language to describe our new family:

> Jesus Christ the faithful witness, the firstborn of the dead, and the ruler of kings on earth.
> To him who loves us and has freed us from our sins by his blood and made us a kingdom, priests to his God and Father, to him be glory and dominion forever and ever. (Rev. 1:5–6)

Why is "firstborn" significant? In the Old Testament, the firstborn son of a family was given special honor and a double share of the father's inheritance. And I am excited to show you why this title is applied to Jesus—get ready to worship!

To wrap our minds around "firstborn" in application to

Jesus, let's think *supreme* in *position* and *inheritance* when we read the word. In Colossians 1:18–19 we are told that Jesus has been given a position of supremacy over all creation: "He is the head of the body, the church. He is the beginning, the firstborn from the dead, that in everything he might be preeminent."

And Jesus certainly deserves to be exalted to the highest place of honor. His divine nature demands such honor, and He is the only One worthy of it. Our sin and *selfishness* crumbled God's original family and good design for the world, but Jesus is restoring God's family, and He accomplished this work through the greatest act of *selflessness*:

> Have this mind among yourselves, which is yours in Christ Jesus, who, though he was in the form of God, did not count equality with God a thing to be grasped, but emptied himself, by taking the form of a servant, being born in the likeness of men. And being found in human form, he humbled himself by becoming obedient to the point of death, even death on a cross. Therefore God has highly exalted him and bestowed on him the name that is above every name, so that at the name of Jesus every knee should bow, in heaven and on earth and under the earth, and every tongue confess that Jesus Christ is Lord, to the glory of God the Father. (Phil. 2:5–11)

Did you notice? Jesus is the firstborn from the dead and is exalted to the highest place of honor over all creation. As a result, every knee will bow and confess that Jesus is Lord over all.

We see this title applied to Jesus again in the messianic Psalm 89. In verse 27, God points forward to Jesus and says, "I will make him the firstborn, the highest of the kings of the earth." In other words, Jesus is the supreme or highest King of the earth. This is why Revelation 1:5 above makes the connection between Jesus as the firstborn from the dead, *and the ruler of kings of earth.*

Let's look at one more place where Jesus is called the firstborn, and then we will bring all of this together:

> And we know that for those who love God all things work together for good, for those who are called according to his purpose. For those whom he foreknew he also predestined to be conformed to the image of his Son, in order that he might be the *firstborn among many brothers.* (Rom. 8:28–29)

Did you catch that last word? Jesus is supreme over all creation and the highest of kings. And yet, God is so abounding in grace that He predestined believers to become Jesus' brothers and sisters! Go ahead and marvel with me. God predestined believers to be part of His family. Jesus Christ the King of kings is called your brother. And He is the model or image our lives are being conformed to reflect. He certainly should have the supreme place of honor in our family.

PARTICIPATING IN THE FAMILY BUSINESS

Now let's return to Revelation 1:5–6 and look at the staggering words John uses to describe *believers*: "To him who loves us and has freed us from our sins by his blood and made us a *kingdom, priests* to his God and Father, to him be glory and dominion forever and ever."

Jesus Christ is the King who is ruling on the worldwide throne. He has freed us from our sin. He has opened the door for each of us to become a member of His royal family. And now we see that He has made us to be a royal priesthood. We are a family who has been given a prominent role to play in the world.

As we have seen, we will rule the world in subjection to God in the Age to Come. But it is amazing to see that Jesus gives each member of His family offices and good works so we can participate in the family business in this age. We are a kingly priesthood who God is using to bring about His plan to re-create the world through the gospel:

> But you are a chosen race, a royal priesthood, a holy nation, a people for his own possession, that you may proclaim the excellencies of him who called you out of darkness into his marvelous light. Once you were not a people, but now you are God's people; once you had not received mercy, but now you have received mercy. (1 Peter 2:9–10)

The word "priesthood" is a rich concept. The privilege and role of a priest was that he was given access to God and was a mediator—going before God on behalf of the people. Jesus is our perfect high priest. There now is no other mediator between us and God. But, *we* can confidently approach God's throne by faith in Jesus (Heb. 4:14–16). In Christ, we have been given access to God to intercede on behalf of others, and we are called to bear witness to Christ's kingship, leading others back to Him.

I hope you are beginning to see that our family business is far greater than buying and selling material goods or influencing political realms. We are given vital offices and roles to use for one central goal; namely, to exalt the firstborn in our family so others will see His glory, repent of their sin, be reconciled back to God, and receive His gift of the kingdom. Our joyful business is making known the excellencies of God who has called us out of darkness into His marvelous light.

I think it is quite thrilling to pause and look at the reflection of this truth in the world around us. Take, for example, the first lady of the United States. By virtue of her marriage or union to the president, she has a role to play in bringing about the welfare of others. In a similar way, by virtue of our union with Christ, we have been given a significant role to play in the universal family business to bring about the welfare of others.

Pause now and consider the realms of influence God has given you to proclaim His excellencies and lead others to Him. Have you ever marveled at the fact that these are opportunities to play an honorable role in the family business? God has called us to be faithful with the realms of influence He has given us in this age, and when He returns, we will rule over the new world with Christ.

BEWARE OF FAMILY RIVALRY

One problem we often see surface within the family business is that we brothers and sisters can be tempted to exalt our own name instead of the name of the firstborn in our family. We can be tempted to seek the special honor and place of Jesus for ourselves. And the result is division, jealousy, covetousness, and sibling rivalry breaking out within our family.

These struggles do not only affect relationships. They also begin to affect the family business. We can begin sinfully exalting and degrading one another based on the specific gifts, services, and activities that God has appointed to each of us (1 Cor. 12). Brothers and sisters can become jealous when someone else is given a *perceivably* bigger platform of influence.

And even leaders can struggle with the same sin, but in a different way. They can begin to use their platform to exalt their own name and perhaps not even realize it until God raises up someone else to lead alongside them—someone they themselves did not ask for. All of a sudden the leader becomes territorial and attempts to use his or her power and influence to keep another brother or sister down. Competition also surfaces between the leaders as each seeks a bigger or more effective ministry than the other.

And what is at the heart of all these sins? We are trying to take the firstborn's place in our family. Thus we should slow down and look this sin in the face so we can see how crazy it is. How could we ever think we could (or should) take Jesus' exalted place of honor? But so it goes with sin and temptation—our mind gets darkened, and we do not see life correctly.

EYES ON HIM

The most effective way to walk in the joy, honor, freedom, and dignity of our family community and business is to keep our affections fired up for the firstborn in our family. The more we worship Him—setting our eyes on Christ's glory and supremacy—the more we will be free to delight in our brothers and sisters when Jesus raises them up to special works of service; and the more we'll be honored to decrease so He may increase (John 3:30). Worshiping the glorious firstborn in our family has become my go-to habit when tempted in these areas of sin.

I specifically remember a day when I saw a thrilling ministry opportunity that some of my sisters got to be part of and I did not. My heart began to slump with disappointment, and all of a sudden I noticed that jealousy was crouching at the door of my heart (Gen. 4:7). By God's grace, the Holy Spirit convicted me and reminded me to worship the firstborn in our family. Thus, I began meditating on some of my favorite pictures of Christ's supremacy such as His victory over Satan during the cosmic battle that took place in the wilderness temptation. Adam and Eve exchanged God for kings, kingdoms, and crowns apart from Him. And so have we. But Jesus defeated Satan by having higher passions and desires for God than the things in this world. And He advanced from the temptation as the One who fights our battles!

Adam and Eve exchanged God for kings, kingdoms, and crowns apart from Him. And so have we. But Jesus defeated Satan . . .

As the Holy Spirit turned the direction of my mind away from self-interest to the pictures of Christ's supremacy that I love in Scripture, it was not long before my lips turned upward into a big smile and I thought, *Oh, how I love our firstborn Brother and King!* He is glorious and should be lifted up high so that all people can see Him and enter into our family. Joy began welling up in my heart. I found myself excited for my sisters to have an opportunity to make our Brother's name known together. And I even began praying for their time to be fruitful for the kingdom.

And guess what . . . all this happened when I was on my way to teach a Bible study myself! Isn't that crazy? God has given each of us gifts, ministries, services, and realms of influence to exalt His name together. And if we are not careful, we can fail to steward our talents and realms of influence with excellence by becoming distracted with what God is doing through others.

There are so many opportunities all around us to make known the excellencies of Christ and to bring others into God's family in our neighborhoods, schools, places of work, and more. We just have to be mindful to look for the kingdom adventures God has set before us and seize them each day for the exaltation of His name!

WHO IS LIKE HIM?

How should we respond to all of this wonderful news? I would like to suggest that we emulate King David when He received the news that God was going to build an everlasting dynasty or royal family through him. In 2 Samuel 7:8 God reminds David of all the things He has done for him: "I took you from the pasture, from following the sheep, that you should be prince over my people Israel."

David had humble roots. He was not a man of great stature or high esteem—not even within his own family. God is pleased to raise up people who do not have an arrogant view of self, but instead love God and seek Him to be their benefactor. Therefore, God was pleased to take David from following sheep and to make him king to rule over and care for God's people.

Then God announced that He was going to do even more in David's life by building a dynasty through Him, "Moreover, the LORD declares to you that the LORD will make you a house" (2 Sam. 7:11). Now look at David's response:

> Then King David went in and sat before the LORD and said, "Who am I, O Lord GOD, and what is my house, that you have brought me thus far? And yet this was a small thing in your eyes, O Lord GOD. You have spoken also of your servant's

house for a great while to come, and this is instruction for mankind, O Lord GoD! . . . Therefore you are great, O LORD God. For there is none like you, and there is no God besides you." (vv. 18–19, 22)

I love when David says there is no one like You, Lord! God brings low the arrogant and lifts up the humble. In 1 Corinthians 1:26–31 we are told that the kind of people God is adopting into His new family have the same humble roots as David. In other words, David's rag-to-riches story is not his alone:

> For consider your calling, brothers: not many of you were wise according to worldly standards, not many were powerful, not many were of noble birth. But God chose what is foolish in the world to shame the wise; God chose what is weak in the world to shame the strong; God chose what is low and despised in the world, even things that are not, to bring to nothing things that are, so that no human being might boast in the presence of God. And because of him you are in Christ Jesus, who became to us wisdom from God, righteousness and sanctification and redemption, so that, as it is written, "Let the one who boasts, boast in the Lord." (1 Cor. 1:26–31)

Since becoming a Christian myself, I have encountered other people from my past who have also heard the gospel and given their life to Jesus. Not many are people who were of high influence, pedigree, or wealth. Of course there are some who were like the apostle Paul—people who possessed high talents and reputations. They, like Paul, have come to see that all of their worldly accomplishments are like dung compared to knowing Christ and have renounced their dependence on such things (Phil. 3:1–11).

But as 1 Corinthians says above, many of them have humble roots. Many come from broken families or have little social status or material wealth, or they were steeped in sin they felt they could never shed. And I cannot even begin to describe to you how my heart explodes with worship when I see the kind of God our Lord is that He is reaching down to help such people. It is amazing to see those who were once downtrodden now have more joy in Christ than those of the world when their money and wine abound (Ps. 4:7).

With such as these—and with you and me—God is building His new dynasty. These are the sons and daughters who will inherit the world and rule with Christ in the Age to Come.

When I see God's grace, compassion, and mercy displayed through His saving work, I join in the choir of praise exulting over our God who "raises up the poor from the dust; he lifts the needy from the ash heap to make them sit with princes and inherit a seat of honor" (1 Sam. 2:8). God is creating a new royal family, and many do not come from the stock that the world would consider powerful, wise, or of important lineage. But God is pleased to save such people because they will look to Him as their help and deliverer. The humble will exult in His name, not their own. In other words, they are primed and ready for the family business!

YOUR FAMILY PORTRAIT

Perhaps when you look at your earthly family portrait you see a family that has been shattered due to divorce, abandonment, abuse, or death. Perhaps you weep when considering the potential of what life could have been like for your family if humanity had not fallen from glory.

But I pray that your tears are beginning to be mingled with hope as well. God is building a new family through Jesus Christ that is absolutely stunning. David was raised up from the pasture to be prince over God's people. And there is a sense in which we can say that this is also true of all believers in Jesus Christ. Jesus is raising up people from the ash heap, adopting us into His royal family, giving us vital roles in the family business now, and will make us sit with princes in the Age to Come, where we will rule and reign with Him.

EXALTING THE FIRSTBORN TOGETHER

1. Do you struggle with wanting to be exalted above your brothers and sisters when you are in a community? Do you become frustrated when others are being honored and lifted up? How do you enter into a community? Do you enter hoping to be exalted or to love others?

   Meditate on the verses in this chapter that talk about Jesus as the firstborn in our family. Perhaps listen to a beautiful worship song that proclaims the excellencies of Christ. Ask Jesus, your glorious Brother, to forgive you for trying to take His place. Then meditate on John the Baptist's joy in decreasing his own public glory to increase the glory of Christ as in John 3:30. Write down ways to enter into community ready to love others as an overflow of your joy in the firstborn of our family.

2. Read Psalm 133. Love, unity, and fellowship with God's people is refreshing and invigorating! What are some ways your sin is causing disunity in the family of God? For example, do you provoke people to jealousy by boasting in subtle ways? Do you judge and criticize others? Do you struggle with covetousness? Are you controlling? What changes can you make to promote unity and refreshing fellowship?

3. Many people feel lonely because they do not have a community or close friends. Can you relate? What are some ways that you can be a change agent? How can you start loving individuals in your church? How can you get involved in someone's life?

How can you generate or join a loving community through your church?

4. Are you struggling with sin or temptation? Please read Hebrews 2:11–18. How does it make you feel to know that Jesus is not ashamed to call you His brother or sister? Jesus did not come to help fallen angels, but the sons of Abraham. He died to deliver you from sin and Satan and to make you holy. How does this encourage you to draw near to our merciful Brother for help?

5. Please read James 2:1–13. God tells us not to commit the sin of showing partiality in the family of God. Take time to consider ways you may show partiality. For example, if you are the leader of a ministry, do you listen to the voice of those who are of meager means as carefully as you listen to those who are wealthy and influential? When you go to a gathering, are you quick to pass by the poor to make friends with those who are finely dressed? In verses 5–6 we are told that God has chosen those who are poor in the world to be rich in faith and heirs of the kingdom. How does seeing poor believers as people who are rich in faith and heirs of the kingdom change your perspective, attitude, and actions?

PART 3

GLORIOUS
REWARD

CHAPTER 9

A MORAL UNIVERSE REFORMED

The nursing child shall play over the hole of the cobra,
and the weaned child shall put his hand on the adder's den.
They shall not hurt or destroy in all my holy mountain; for
the earth shall be full of the knowledge of the LORD as the
waters cover the sea.

—Isaiah 11:8–9

One summer my husband, Bobby, and I taught in a seminary in Africa. Bobby provided biblical education to African pastors, and I devoted my time to teaching their wives. The day we presented a summary of church history, we were taken aback by the excitement that filled the room.

When we inquired into the students' enthusiasm, they began sharing stories about the corruption of pastors and church leaders in their particular communities. Many of their stories revolved around leaders who, rather than promoting the gospel, were using their authority in sinful ways such as sleeping with congregants and swindling money (of course, not all African churches are corrupt—I am merely referring to the communities that our students were in at the time).

So you can imagine the setting—right? The corruption and injustice these people were encountering had caused their hearts to become kindling wood all around us. And unbeknownst to us, when we began to teach about what the gospel actually means and how the gospel ignited a reformation throughout the church in the 1500s, it was as if a match was dropped in the room. Then, wildfires of worship broke out before our eyes!

The students were in awe of the gospel and what God is doing in the lives of those who believe. They were inspired by reformers who stood up for the truth in order to lead others to salvation. And they were filled with the hope of what life could be like when corruption is replaced with the truth, righteousness, and beauty of God. I could not help but see that moment as a small preview of the day when Jesus will reform the world and the praise that will erupt from the hearts of believers.

Let's walk through some vivid passages in the Bible that describe the time when Jesus will reform the world by bringing all things in submission to Him. Consider with me what it will be like when evil, sin, and wickedness exist no more. Let's fire up our imaginations for what it will be like when believers inherit the earth and begin cultivating the world together for the glory of God. Goodness, truth, and beauty will be everywhere!

And for the sake of your worship, keep in mind that all these things will happen because of who Jesus is. Our coming King is a victorious warrior who loves righteousness and hates wickedness. And now we will see how these aspects of the King will give shape to the world and to the lives of all people.

SEVERE PICTURES

In Genesis 3, humanity rebelled against God. We wanted to determine for ourselves what is right from what is wrong, what is good from what is evil. As a result, we threw off God's good limits. The result is a world where some people think it is right to have an affair; where some people think it is right to have an abortion; where some people think it is right to have sex with children; where some people think it is right to turn a blind eye to sin in order to protect a friend or a family member; where systemic injustice is set in place to keep entire ethnic groups at a disadvantage; where some people are enslaved and trafficked—the list of corruption and oppression goes on and on. But Isaiah 24 says God will judge the world because people have broken His laws and corrupted the good world He has made (vv. 4–5).

Psalm 2 describes the worldwide opposition against the Lord and His Anointed King. But the psalm goes on to describe the King's defeat of the wicked in severe terms. Jesus will return and end the rebellion against Him. He will "break" the nations with a "rod of iron" and "dash them in pieces" (v. 9). Psalm 110:5b–7 gives us another severe and graphic picture of Jesus as our warrior King:

> He will shatter kings on the day of his wrath. He will execute judgment among the nations, filling them with corpses; he will shatter the chiefs over the wide earth. He will drink from the brook by the way; therefore he will lift up his head.

This prophetic picture is quite different from the image of Jesus dying bloody on the cross to pay for the sin of rebels. Jesus is the Lamb of God, but we must remember that He is also the Lion of Judah (Rev. 5:5). Many of us may not be familiar with Jesus as the warrior King. So let's take a closer look at what will unfold when the warrior King defeats His enemies through cataclysmic judgments upon the world.

THE WARRIOR KING

In Isaiah 24 the word "earth" is used multiple times. The point is hard to miss. God wants us to know that judgment is coming upon the whole earth and that no one will escape. Many biblical commentators believe that Isaiah 24 looks forward to the tribulation as described in Revelation 6, when Jesus takes the scroll or title deed to the universe and begins breaking the seals, which unleashes God's judgment on the earth. God is going to level all society.[1] In other words, there will be no advantage to being a religious leader, the head of a successful company, or the most socially prominent in a community. Furthermore, God will not turn a blind eye to the rebellion of the underprivileged. They will be held accountable for their sin as well:

> Behold, the LORD will empty the earth and make it desolate, and he will twist its surface and scatter its inhabitants. And it shall be, as with the people, so with the priest; as with the slave, so with his master; as with the maid, so with her mistress; as with the buyer, so with the seller; as with the lender, so with the borrower; as with the creditor, so with the debtor. The earth shall be utterly empty and utterly plundered; for the LORD has spoken this word.
>
> The earth mourns and withers; the world languishes

and withers; the highest people of the earth languish. The earth lies defiled under its inhabitants; for they have transgressed the laws, violated the statues, broken the everlasting covenant. (Isa. 24:1–5)

This passage should get our attention. Perhaps you have been shown favor throughout your life because you are physically beautiful, talented, successful, wealthy, from a renowned family, or have charisma. Or perhaps you have been shown mercy and assistance because you are poor and underprivileged. God warns us in advance that none of these things will save us from His coming wrath against sin. The Lord is going to judge the world because we have broken His laws and defiled the good world He made. And everyone who does not repent of their sin and put their faith in Jesus Christ in this age of grace will bear the consequences for their sin and guilt.

Bobby and I lived in Louisville, Kentucky, for one year. During our short time there we looked forward to experiencing some elements of the Kentucky Derby. However, my enthusiasm was dampened when a local advocate reminded me of the sad side of many celebrations in our fallen world such as the Derby, Super Bowl, and state fairs; namely, sex traffickers bring in many women and children to meet increased demands at some of the big parties. It is sad to consider the joy fallen people have in wickedness and how people can party and revel in other people's pain. But when Jesus——who hates wickedness—brings judgment upon the earth, the music will stop, the parties will cease, and there will be no more joy or gladness in wickedness:

The wine mourns, the vine languishes, all the merry-hearted sigh. The mirth of the tambourines is stilled, the noise of the jubilant has ceased, the mirth of the lyre is stilled. No more do they drink wine with singing; strong drink is bitter to those who drink it. The wasted city is broken down; every house is shut up so that none can enter. There is an outcry in the streets for lack of wine; all joy has grown dark; the gladness of the earth is banished. Desolation is left in the city; the gates are battered into ruins. For thus it shall be in the midst of the earth among the nations, as when an olive tree is beaten, as at the gleaning when the grape harvest is done. (Isa. 24:7–13)

Have you ever seen a reformer step onto a scene and begin reshaping the world around you? I remember a time when there was widespread corruption in an arena of our life. The oppression became heavy under the leadership of corrupt people, the injustice was maddening, and anxiety was a constant spiritual battle. But then one day a courageous man was raised to leadership. It was so thrilling to see someone take a stand against the corrupt leaders who lived for their own self-interest instead of serving those under their leadership.

My heart exploded with joy when the reformer took the mantle of leadership. I was in awe to see how quickly he began cleaning house by removing corrupt people from their places of authority and replacing them with people who had good moral values. Peace and freedom flooded my soul because the fear of oppression was removed for a time. And once again, I marveled knowing God was giving me another small preview to savor in anticipation of His coming judgment and deliverance.

When our King begins breaking oppressive regimes, corrupt systems of power, and self-serving leaders, God's people will erupt with ecstatic, celebratory shouts. I'm sure it will be quite stunning to see because many of the corrupt leaders in this fallen world seem like unmovable pillars due to their power, wealth, and/or influence. And believers will exult in His power and majesty:

> They lift up their voices, they sing for joy; over the majesty of the LORD they shout from the west. Therefore in the east give glory to the LORD; in the coastlands of the sea, give glory to the name of the LORD, the God of Israel. From the ends of the earth we hear songs of praise, of glory to the Righteous One. (Isa. 24:14–16)

THE WICKED ENSNARED

Christ's incredible power and majesty will be exerted to end the rebellion against Him and to deliver the oppressed, which will be beautiful to believers (2 Thess. 1:10). But that same power and wrath will be terrifying to the wicked:

> Terror and the pit and the snare are upon you, O inhabitant of the earth! He who flees at the sound of the terror shall fall into the pit, and he who climbs out of the pit shall be caught in the snare. For the windows of heaven are opened, and the foundations of the earth tremble. The earth is utterly broken, the earth is split apart, the earth is violently shaken. The earth staggers like a drunken man; it sways like a hut;

its transgression lies heavy upon it, and it falls, and will not rise again. (Isa. 24:17–20)

The Lord's coming judgment will be horrifying for unbelievers. God uses the language of an animal trying to flee from a hunter. The "sound of the terror" reminds us of the sound hunters make to scare their game and drive them into their snares. When God's judgment comes, people will be like animals trying to escape but will be unable to do so because they will fall into a pit. And even if they are able to climb out of one pit, they will be caught in another snare. In other words, one catastrophe after another will befall them.[2]

OUR REFUGE WHEN THE EARTH GIVES WAY

It is sobering to consider the turn of fortunes that will take place for the unrepentant. God originally made the world as a safe and welcoming home. But God will turn our habitat against the unrepentant inhabitants of the earth by causing natural disasters to punish and destroy them. We are told that the "windows of heaven" will be opened (v. 18). This phrase recalls the great flood that God caused to come upon the earth in the days of Noah when "the great deep burst forth, and the windows of the heavens were opened" (Gen. 7:11). There will also be great earthquakes that will cause the earth to stagger like a drunk man and sway like a hut in a storm. People will be destroyed, and this present earth will fall, never to rise again.

I am writing this chapter the week that Hurricane Harvey hit the Texas coast and has been hovering over Houston, causing catastrophic flooding and tornadoes throughout the city.

As you can imagine, these scenes are bringing these truths vividly alive.

The hurricane developed fast, and we did not have much advance warning. The morning I began to realize the severity of the coming storm, I also recognized the difficulty of evacuating because the roads were already congested with people who were leaving the coastal areas. As a result, I knew I needed to get supplies as quickly as I could.

The big chain stores in Houston were already sold out of many necessities. But my husband was able to locate an obscure hardware store in the city. Since Bobby had to go to work in the morning, Jade and I set off to find supplies. We arrived at the store thirty minutes before it opened and joined the line already forming.

It was humbling to stand side by side with others and recognize together how small and dependent we are on resources outside of ourselves. When the manager arrived, he announced that no more trucks would be coming into the Houston area because none of the drivers wanted to be in the path of the storm. As a result, the store only had enough generators to sell to those who arrived before the doors opened. People started stirring with selfishness in a frightening way, but the managers were prepared to maintain a sense of order.

Grateful to be able to find the items on our list, Jade and I wheeled up our cart to the counter to pay. But right when I gave the checker my card, the system went down. Everyone in line looked at one another, concerned, because most of us did not have cash. I closed my eyes and began to pray. By God's grace, the system came up for a window of time, allowing us to make our purchases. As we loaded up our car I felt a deep sense of gratitude for having found what we needed, but I also knew that we were facing another challenge.

Generators run on gas. And almost all the gas stations were running out of fuel. Jade and I began to pray again. After trying several stations to no avail, we stumbled on another obscure store with just a little gas left. The remaining gas sputtered and spit into our tanks, filling them to the top. And as we headed home with everything we needed to wait out the storm, there was an eerie feeling as the streets of our busy city became desolate and necessary resources for survival began to run out.

Despite the warnings of the upcoming storm, some people laughed at the forecasters, thinking that they were embellishing details to create media hype. But when the rain came, it was as if the windows of heaven were opened because it just didn't stop falling. And as the waters continued to rise, this laughter began to cease. Rivers and bayous began to flood their banks, causing mandatory evacuations throughout the city. And there was a growing sense of desperation throughout as houses began taking on water, forcing people out into the dangerous flood waters that were filled with contamination, rubbish, snakes, and alligators.

At home I began to seek the Lord. It was one of those moments when God reminds you of His ever-abiding presence. I opened my Bible to Psalm 46, which says, "God is our refuge and strength, a very present help in trouble. Therefore we will not fear though the earth gives way, though the mountains be moved into the heart of the sea, though its waters roar and foam, though the mountains tremble at its swelling" (vv. 1–3).

As you can imagine, I was in awe of how perfect this verse was in the moment. Jesus reminded me that He is like a fortress or a high and safe place for those who trust in Him, even through perils and natural disasters. But I quickly realized this psalm is not

There are times when we cry out, "How long, oh Lord?" But there is a day coming soon when we will realize all that we have longed for and we will exult with loud triumphal cheers that He is faithful!

merely talking about perils in the here and now. It is also pointing forward to the final and climactic day of the LORD.[3] The rest of Psalm 46 goes on to say:

There is a river whose streams make glad the city of God, the holy habitation of the Most High. God is in the midst of her; she shall not be moved; God will help her when morning dawns. The nations rage, the kingdoms totter; he utters his voice, the earth melts. The LORD of hosts is with us; the God of Jacob is our fortress.

Come, behold the works of the LORD, how he has brought desolations on the earth. He makes wars cease to the end of the earth; he breaks the bow and shatters the spear; he burns the chariots with fire. "Be still, and know that I am God. I will be exalted among the nations, I will be exalted in the earth!" The LORD of hosts is with us; the God of Jacob is our fortress. (vv. 4–11)

Even when this present evil world falls—and as we have seen in Isaiah 24:20, it will fall never to rise again—God will be present to help His people. Throughout the hurricane God protected us in a gracious way. And since I was writing this chapter at the same time, I could not help but be reminded of God's coming judgment. He will bring desolations on the earth. Laughter and music will cease. People will be destroyed. But He will protect those who trust in Him by obeying His instructions for salvation through Jesus Christ. God will judge the world. But He will be a mighty refuge and salvation for those who trust in Him!

THE INAUGURATION OF THE AGE TO COME

Now let's see how the rest of Isaiah 24 and 25 unfold. After God brings desolations on the earth, He will gather the unrepentant together as prisoners and shut them up in prison as they await the final judgment at the great white throne, where they will be condemned for their sins and punished forever (Rev. 20:11–15). Then He will manifest His good reign throughout the earth:

> On that day the LORD will punish the host of heaven, in heaven, and the kings of the earth, on the earth. They will be gathered together as prisoners in a pit; they will be shut up in a prison, and after many days they will be punished. Then the moon will be confounded and the sun ashamed, for the LORD of hosts reigns on Mount Zion and in Jerusalem, and his glory will be before his elders. (Isa. 24:21–23)

After sin and corruption is removed from the earth, the redeemed will break out in praise, joy, and deep celebration over the liberation of the world by our Hero and Savior, Jesus Christ. "LORD, you are my God; I will exalt you; I will praise your name, for you have done wonderful things, plans formed of old, faithful and sure" (Isa. 25:1). Did you hear all the rich words that will come from our hearts on that day? We are going to be in awe when we step into the realization of all the wonderful things God promised long ago.

Perhaps I will remember the summer I wrote this book, hovering over the promises of God concerning the Age to Come and marvel at His faithfulness to bring all these things to pass. And perhaps you will remember the times in your life when you stood on God's promises through suffering, considering the wonderful things to come.

Verse 9 says, "It will be said on that day, 'Behold, this is our God; we have waited for him, that he might save us. This is the LORD; we have waited for him; let us be glad and rejoice in his salvation.'" I love this verse, because there are times when even believers begin to question the promises of God. And there are times when we cry out, "How long, oh Lord?" But there is a day coming soon when we will realize all that we have longed for and we will exult with loud triumphal cheers that He is faithful!

FESTIVE FELLOWSHIP—AND FINE DINING

In Isaiah 25:2–5 the Holy Spirit gives us another glimpse of more precious sentiments that will flow from our hearts. The word "ruthless" is repeated three times, emphasizing the love we will experience for Jesus when we see Him execute justice on the ruthless, resulting in the deliverance of the poor, needy, and distressed. Our celebration over our King's faithfulness and deliverance is then followed in verse 6 by a picture of believers attending a lavish banquet hosted by Jesus! It is thrilling to anticipate the rich fellowship and fine dining we will experience together on the mountain of the Lord.

Bobby and I have a group of friends we connect with on a deep level. Some of my sweetest memories with them are when we sit at a round table in a restaurant by a fireplace and share life and laughter together over good food. The sense of connection, love, belonging, and goodwill toward one another is refreshing and invigorating. I can hardly imagine how rich our relationships will be in the Age to Come. I can hardly imagine how rich our relationships with be in the Age to Come. God will swallow up death for all who are in attendance! In other words, we will become immortal:

> And he will swallow up on this mountain the covering that is cast over all peoples, the veil that is spread over all nations. He will swallow up death forever; and the Lord GOD will wipe away tears from all faces, and the reproach of his people he will take away from all the earth, for the LORD has spoken. It will be said on that day, "Behold, this is our God; we have waited for him, that he might save us. This is the LORD; we have waited for him; let us be glad and rejoice in his salvation." (Isa. 25:7–9)

UNIVERSAL PEACE

After Jesus brings judgment upon the earth, the Prince of Peace will create universal peace in His kingdom. It is absolutely stunning to envision the world operating according to God's good design:

> The wolf shall dwell with the lamb, and the leopard shall lie down with the young goat, and the calf and the lion and the fattened calf together; and a little child shall lead them. The cow and the bear shall graze; their young shall lie down together; and the lion shall eat straw like the ox. The nursing child shall play over the hole of the cobra, and the weaned child shall put his hand on the adder's den. They shall not hurt or destroy in all my holy mountain; for the earth shall be full of the knowledge of the LORD as the waters cover the sea.
>
> In that day the root of Jesse, who shall stand as a signal for the peoples—of him shall the nations inquire, and his resting place shall be glorious. (Isa. 11:6–10)

Can you imagine? Can you imagine what it will be like to see Jesus as a courageous Reformer when He removes all the corrupt people and pillars in the world? Can you imagine what it will be like when sin and wickedness is wiped away? Can you imagine what it will be like to look up and down the city streets and through the fields, only to see believers in Jesus Christ?

Can you imagine standing in a bright new day in a beautiful new world where creation seems to be alive all around you? when animals are not a threat to you at all? what it will be to feel deeply connected in intimacy and joy with the new family of God? or to set off on new adventures with loved ones in a world of wonder without fear of harm or death?

Can you imagine what it will be like when everyone begins to create technology, art, music, and culture to celebrate God and

His beautiful design for life? God's goodness, beauty, and truth will be everywhere!

PREVIEWS OF THE COMING JUDGMENT

There are many natural disasters that take place in our midst, such as Hurricane Harvey, which can be catastrophic and life threatening. These moments provide us with sobering previews of the Lord's coming judgment upon the earth. We were so relieved the morning we woke up and realized the rain had stopped and the water was finally beginning to recede. We had made it through the long weekend!

But it was sobering to realize that relief will never come to the unrepentant on the day of the Lord. The door into the kingdom of God will be closed. And it will be horrifying for people to realize that their life will not merely be snuffed out like a candle. Instead they will be gathered together as prisoners and be punished for age upon age without end.

But God graciously uses natural disasters in this age to humble people and bring them to salvation before He returns. Therefore, we can seize catastrophes as great moments of hope for gospel opportunities. And God will be with us to do powerful kingdom works. One day during the hurricane there was a break in the rain, so we began visiting our neighbors to see if they needed anything.

One woman needed dialysis but, due to the flooding, there was no way out of our neighborhood, and if she was unable to get to a clinic she could go into a coma. The emergency lines were so busy with similar situations throughout the city that no one was responding to her calls. We called upon God through prayer and then spent more time talking with her family. Before we left, she received a phone call from a medical rescue team saying they were on their way to get her!

We all rejoiced together in God's gracious response to our prayer. And not just in this incident. It was amazing to see God disperse believers all throughout Houston for hands-on help, as well as sharing the gospel and leading people to salvation.

Let's make the most of our opportunities in this present age of grace while awaiting the Age to Come!

PARTICIPATING IN THE
POWER OF THE NEW AGE NOW

1. Spend time meditating on the severe pictures of Jesus as a warrior who will morally reform the world. Write down the names of unbelievers in your life you would like to share the gospel with. Some years ago my husband was meditating on the severe warnings in the Bible, which motivated him to write one of his family members a letter out of love, communicating the severity of judgment and hell. He concluded the letter by pleading with his family member to come to salvation. Through that initiative, the man's entire household repented of their sin and began a new life with Christ. Their lives have been transformed in beautiful ways!

2. We are still waiting for the second coming of our warrior King and His moral reformation of the universe. However, He has furnished believers with His divine power and magnificent promises in this age to escape the corruption in this world that is caused by evil desires. In other words, the Holy Spirit is already reforming believers' lives! Reflect on 2 Peter 1:4 and Romans 6:6, 12, 14.

3. Let's take hold of the power of the new age by actively participating in our transformation. Colossians 3:9–10 says Christians still have an ability to sin (our old self in Adam), but we also have the ability to obey God (our new self in Christ). Thus, we are called to put off the attitudes and actions of our old self and replace them with the attitudes and actions of Christ. Read 1 Corinthians 6:9–11. Make a list

of your old self patterns of sin that you are still walking in, repent, and begin cultivating new Christlike attitudes and actions (Gal. 2:20). Picture, ponder, and pray over these Christlike characteristics in the morning and before bed.

4. Read 2 Thessalonians 1:5–12. How does Christ's coming vengeance upon those who afflict you free you from the temptation to seek vengeance yourself and strengthen you to persevere through suffering for the sake of righteousness?

5. Meditate on the glorious pictures of life under the reign of Jesus Christ. Which ones are the most comforting to you during your current season of life and why?

CHAPTER 10

LOYALISTS CROWNED

"Behold, I am coming quickly, and My reward is with Me, to render to every man according to what he has done."
—Revelation 22:12 NASB

When a leader of a government steps into high office, he often rewards his loyal followers by giving them public commendation and honorable offices to represent him.

Believers in Jesus Christ are His loyalists. Though there is worldwide opposition to Jesus, His faithful followers stand for Him, being ridiculed, mocked, and even persecuted for their association with Him. But when Christ returns and manifests His rule throughout the earth, we will see Him do another gracious work. He will richly reward His loyalists with the privilege of living with Him, public commendation, crowns of honor, and platforms to rule as His representatives throughout the new world!

This will take place when all believers appear before the judgment seat of Christ and are recompensed for our deeds done in this life, whether good or bad.[1] And in view of the coming assessment, Paul tells us that we should make it our aim in life to please God:

> So whether we are at home or away, we make it our aim to please him. For we must all appear before the judgment

179

seat of Christ, so that each one may receive what is due for what he has done in the body, whether good or evil. (2 Cor. 5:9–10)

It is important to note that this evaluation does not determine one's salvation. As Ephesians 2:8–9 explains, believers are saved by grace through faith, not our own good works. But believers will give an account for our obedience in this life and be rewarded accordingly.

The term "judgment seat" comes from the Greek word *bema*. This word is used in Matthew 27:19 to describe the place where Pontius Pilate judged Jesus. And the word is also used to describe "an elevated platform where victorious athletes went to receive their crowns."[2] Thus, the judgment seat describes the place where Jesus will evaluate our deeds done while in the body and reward us accordingly.

This is both exciting and frightening. It is exciting for believers to consider this from the perspective of C. S. Lewis in The Chronicles of Narnia, when Aslan rewards the sons of Adam and the daughters of Eve with new names of honor, crowns, and thrones. But it is also frightening to consider this from the perspective of what Lewis describes as the "naked idea of Judgment."[3] That being said, I think Lewis is right to suggest that the importance of reckoning with the coming judgment is not ultimately how it makes us feel, but that we live in view of it.

THE WORLD'S LAST NIGHT

C. S. Lewis's "The World's Last Night" is an essay about the second coming of Christ. This title was taken from a poem written by John Donne, in which he discusses how we should live if the world were ending today. Lewis says the biblical passages concerning the second return of Jesus Christ have not had their proper work in our lives if they do not make us live in the light of Donne's question, "What if this present were the world's last night?"

Lewis argues that the importance of this question does not terminate on the emotional effects it has on us—whether it causes us to be excited or afraid. Emotions cannot be sustained. The significance of this question is that it causes us to always take the End into account.

What is essential to keep in mind is that when this world comes to an end, we will all face judgment. Thus, we should "train ourselves to ask more and more often how the thing which we are saying or doing (or failing to do) at each moment will look when the irresistible light streams in upon it" at the judgment. Those who are faithfully fulfilling God's will and doing His business when He returns will be happy to meet Him in this way.[4]

We have talked throughout this book about the obedience of faith in the context of taking the adventure of new life with Christ. And I believe this is a fitting context—following the King into His glorious kingdom *is* the supreme adventure of life.

But it is also important for us to recognize that the call to take the supreme adventure comes from the *King*. In other words, God is sovereign. When He calls people to do something, we must obey. And there are consequences for refusing Him. A powerful example is in Isaiah 1:18–20: "Come now, let us reason together, says the LORD: though your sins are like scarlet, they shall be as white as snow . . . if you are willing and obedient, you shall eat the good of the land; but if you refuse and rebel, you shall be eaten by the sword." In a similar way, God offers to for-

God offers to forgive us for our sin and bring us into the good life with Him! Those who receive His gift of salvation will enjoy a glorious life.

give us for our sin through Jesus Christ and bring us into the good life with Him! Those who receive His gift of salvation will enjoy a glorious life. But those who refuse will suffer eternal destruction away from His presence forever.

Now the judgment of believers will not pertain to our salvation. But even believers will be reminded of His sovereign lordship over our lives because we will give an account for our obedience to our King's commands, and we will receive or lose eternal rewards accordingly. So let's take a closer look at how God's grace, our obedience of faith, and eternal rewards work together.

CHARACTER AND CONDUCT

Following His victory over Satan (Matt. 4:1–11), Jesus is filled with the Holy Spirit and begins preaching, "Repent, for the kingdom of heaven is at hand" (4:17). Jesus calls His first followers to leave behind their old life and follow Him (4:18–22), and then the narrative takes us to His Sermon on the Mount, where He begins teaching about the character and conduct of kingdom citizens (chapters 5–7).[5]

In this well-known passage, we see Jesus as a master teacher! He wonderfully combines the themes of salvation by grace, the obedience of faith, and rewards together in a cohesive way. Jesus shows the high standard of righteousness required to enter into the kingdom—namely, moral perfection (Matt. 5:48). He uses God's law to show sinners our need for Him. By pointing to our inability to keep God's law, Jesus reveals that we are unable to enter into the kingdom through human effort and meritorious works.

But He opens His sermon by pointing sinners to the way we can enter into the kingdom; specifically, by receiving it as a gift of divine grace: "Blessed are the poor in spirit, for theirs is the kingdom of heaven" (5:3). Those who realize our spiritual bankruptcy and inability to earn salvation by our own effort and works can receive the kingdom of God as a gift.

Christ closes His message by saying there are two gates or ways. One leads to destruction, but the other leads to the destiny we all long for (7:13–14). The gate that allows us to enter into the kingdom is narrow; namely, submission to Jesus Christ as our King and obedience to Him (Matt. 7:21–23).

So we see that Jesus gives a thorough lesson on salvation, which is filled out with more detail throughout the rest of the New Testament. No one can enter the kingdom of God by performing works of the law. If we stumble even at one point, we have sinned, and are guilty of breaking the law (James 2:10).

But Jesus perfectly obeyed the law. And by grace, God applies the perfect moral record of Jesus to the lives of those who trust in Him for salvation. "By the one man's obedience the many will be made righteous" (Rom. 5:19). Thus, salvation is by grace through faith, not by performing works of the law. "For by grace you have been saved through faith. And this is not your own doing; it is the gift of God, not a result of works, so that no one may boast" (Eph. 2:8–9). Those who renounce self-sufficiency and self-righteousness and receive Christ's gift of salvation will enter into the kingdom of God.

Now, are you ready for this? Once a woman receives the gift of salvation, then she *will* begin to produce good works through her life. Jesus said we will know who belongs to Christ and His kingdom by their fruit or works. "A good tree cannot produce bad fruit, nor can a bad tree produce good fruit" (Matt. 7:18 NASB).

The apostle Paul echoes this truth. Right after telling us that we are saved by grace through faith, not good works, Paul goes on to say we were saved *for* good works: "For we are his workmanship, created in Christ Jesus for good works, which God prepared beforehand, that we should walk in them" (Eph. 2:10). God's grace working in the lives of believers *will* begin transforming us to become people who are zealous to perform good works:

> For the grace of God has appeared, bringing salvation for all people, training us to renounce ungodliness and worldly passions, and to live self-controlled, upright, and godly lives in the present age, waiting for our blessed hope, the appearing of the glory of our great God and Savior Jesus Christ, who gave himself for us to redeem us from all lawlessness and to purify for himself a people for his own possession who are zealous for good works. (Titus 2:11–14)

Thus, Jesus begins teaching us in the Sermon on the Mount how to enter into the kingdom of God—namely, through Him. He also teaches that believers will become lights in the world so that when people see the beautiful character of God through our attitudes and good works, they will give glory to God—the one who produces these works in our lives (Matt. 5:14–16).

Present and Future Rewards

In the middle of Jesus' message, He teaches on the character and conduct that will be produced in people's lives by His saving grace (Matt. 5–7). And He weaves the concept of rewards within it! There are present and future rewards for those who love Christ and obey Him by faith.

We are to be gentle, merciful, pure in heart, peacemakers, to persevere through persecution, and more (5:4–11). And by doing so, we will receive rewards such as inheriting the earth, mercy from the King, the ability to see God, and being called sons of God.

We are to be people who do not harbor anger or lust in our hearts (vv. 21–30).

We are not to divorce (vv. 31–32).

We are to be careful about what we say we'll do, keep our word, restrain ourselves from retaliation, and show love toward our enemies (vv. 33–48).

We are to practice righteousness by giving to the poor, praying, and fasting with a genuine spirit in secret rather than being a showboat. And when we practice our righteousness in humility and authenticity, "your Father who sees in secret will reward you" (6:4).

I do not need to spend much time discussing why living in these ways is a reward in itself. It is a great reward to be set free from our sin and to be able to participate in the divine life (2 Peter 1:4). Our present day reward is not being overcome with anger or lust. We can enjoy the reward of courageous love now. We can experience the reward of communing with the Father through prayer and being part of advancing Christ's kingdom throughout the world (Matt. 6:5–15).

But Jesus also points to more rewards that will be given to His people in the Age to Come for loving and obeying Him in this life. For example, Jesus tells us to rejoice when we are persecuted for His name because our "reward is great in heaven" (5:11–12). Concerning wealth, Jesus teaches us to not store up for ourselves treasures on earth but "lay up for yourselves treasures in heaven . . . for where your treasure is, there your heart will be also" (6:20–21).

And so we see that Christ's teaching in the Sermon on the Mount is thorough and filled out with more detail through the rest of the New Testament. A person does not enter the kingdom of God by performing good works of her own. She enters the kingdom of God by faith in God's grace. We will not reach perfection until the Age to Come. But God's grace is at work in our lives, enabling us to become more like Him each day: "His divine power has given us everything we need for a godly life through our knowledge of him who called us by his own glory and goodness" (2 Peter 1:3 NIV).

God has graciously given us incentives to keep us moving out of our sinful tendencies to participate in the glorious new life with Him.

Knowing the King, being conformed into His likeness, and participating in the advancement of His kingdom is its own present day reward. But Jesus wants us to know that He will also reward us for loving and obeying Him in this life with eternal rewards at the judgment seat of Christ. Thus, Scripture teaches that our progress in kingdom character and conduct does not only have value for today but also for the Age to

Come: "godliness is of value in every way, as it holds promise for the present life and also for the life to come" (1 Tim. 4:8).

MEANT TO MOTIVATE!

All this talk about rewards is meant to motivate us, the bride of Christ, to seek Him more fully. After I was spiritually born again by faith, I began to thirst for righteousness. It was such a strange experience to not merely want to seek God for His blessings, but to actually want to know Him and become more like Him. I loved my new church and doing life with the people of God. But I felt unholy in their presence.

Though God had made me righteous in position before Him by applying Christ's righteousness to my life by faith, different areas of my life reflected the wisdom of the world. As a result, I spent many nights in the church chapel after everyone else had gone home praying with loud cries and tears for God to make me holy in practice like Him. I wouldn't have known at the time what to call this experience, but later I realized it is the thirst for righteousness that God implants into the heart of His people.

My heart was set on becoming more like Christ. As Jesus so fittingly describes it, I was "hungering" and "thirsting" to know God's love and to become like Him by loving others in free and courageous ways. And God was gracious. He began conforming my life little by little by the power of the Holy Spirit through the Scriptures and the church (2 Cor. 3:18).

But there have also been times in my Christian life when I needed more motivation to persevere in Christ's character and conduct. When sin begins to obscure our vision, we're not as motivated to become like Christ. But God has graciously given us other incentives to keep us moving out of our sinful tendencies to participate in the glorious new life with Him—one of these is the judgment seat of Christ.

Remembering that I will have to give an account to Christ for a fleeting moment of selfishness is very motivating—Amen? Jesus talks about rewards in relation to our character and conduct. And He also talks about rewards in relation to the stewardship of our gifts.

KINGDOM BUSINESS

Jesus' disciples thought He would set up His kingdom immediately. In order to clear up their confusion, Jesus told them a story revealing more insight on the obedience of faith and eternal rewards:

> A nobleman went into a far country to receive for himself a kingdom and then return. Calling ten of his servants, he gave them ten minas, and said to them, "Engage in business until I come." (Luke 19:12–13)

Before the nobleman's departure, he gave each of his servants one mina, which is a unit of money, and told them to engage in his business until his return. Jesus is the King of noble birth who has gone to heaven to receive His kingdom. He will return to manifest His rule throughout the world. Until that time, He has given each of us gifts and opportunities to advance His kingdom. And the Great Commission is our task (Matt. 28:18–20).

Jesus reveals in this passage that stewards must be found faithful when He returns. And this, of course is not a foreign concept to us. When you hire a babysitter, you expect her to be faithful in managing your household and children according to your instructions while you are away. No one wants to return home and see the children in disarray while the babysitter is occupied with her smartphone! We expect her to be faithful to the job we have given her.

Jesus has given us grace gifts and works of service to do until He returns (1 Cor. 12). And we will give account for our diligence or lack of it. Let's see how the king's servants did when he returned:

> When he returned, having received the kingdom, he ordered these servants to whom he had given the money to be called to him, that he might know what they had gained by doing business. The first came before him, saying, "Lord, your mina has made ten minas more." And he said to him, "Well done, good servant! Because you have been faithful in a very little, you shall have authority over ten cities." And the second came, saying, "Lord, your mina has made five minas." And he said to him, "And you are to be over five cities." (Luke 19:15–19)

Notice that the first two faithful servants acknowledged that the minas that produced a return had been given to them— "Lord, *your* mina has made ten minas more" (vv. 16, 18). Likewise, our good works are produced by the power of God's grace at work in our lives. But we will be held accountable for being diligent with these gifts and graces.[6]

The apostle Paul describes it this way: "By the grace of God I am what I am, and his grace toward me was not in vain. On the contrary, I worked harder than any of them, though it was not I, but the grace of God that is with me" (1 Cor. 15:10). Paul knew God's grace was the power at work in His life to produce good works. And so Paul was diligent to work hard for God's glory.

The first two servants are representations of genuine believers. And both were welcomed into the joy of their Master! This is an important point. Both entered into eternal joy in the presence of their King. Both were richly rewarded. But there were different degrees of reward based on their diligence. Some of us can be deceived by thinking that those in the body of Christ who have what we might consider greater gifts and great influence will receive greater eternal rewards. But Jesus reveals in this passage that the rewards are not based on gifts and opportunities, but rather that we are faithful with the gifts and opportunities He has given us.

These opportunities will change based on the season of life we are in. There have been seasons where God has called me to be busy about using my gifts in formal ministry positions such as writing or teaching at women's events. But there have also been times when He called me to shift gears to focus on my family. And during those times I used my gifts more in my neighborhood and Jade's schools.

The faithful first two servants were rewarded. What about the third?

> Then another came, saying, "Lord, here is your mina, which I kept laid away in a handkerchief; for I was afraid of you, because you are a severe man. You take what you did not deposit, and reap what you did not sow." He said to him, "I will condemn you with your own words, you wicked servant! You

knew that I was a severe man, taking what I did not deposit and reaping what I did not sow? . . . Take the mina away from him, and give it to the one who has the ten minas." And they said to him, "Lord, he has ten minas!" "I tell you that to everyone who has, more will be given, but from the one who has not, even what he has will be taken away. But as for these enemies of mine, who did not want me to reign over them, bring them here and slaughter them before me." (Luke 19:20–27)

The last servant provides a wake-up call for any who are lingering in the church, saying the things believers say, doing the things believers do, but who do not really love the Lord or want Him to rule over them!

MIDLIFE HARVEST: A MIDLIFE GRACE

One hard blessing at midlife is that people begin to see the harvest of their decisions come in.[8] It is the strangest thing and can come on you suddenly. It is as if one day you are walking through the field of your life—the same field you have lived in and walked through for years. But then one day you realize the field is no longer bare. Crops are growing up around you; your decisions and actions over time have borne fruit.

A couple who neglected their marriage is beginning to reap selfishness, and their marriage is falling apart. A woman who has been eating unhealthy food for twenty years discovers that her poor habits have finally taken their toll, and she has a systemic disease. A person who looked at her career as her primary way of making an impact on the world is weeping with regret as

Midlife grace . . . an early wake up call, a sober reminder at the midpoint of our journey that the principle of sowing and reaping applies to us all.

her adult children are estranged from her.

And even the woman who has sought to diligently learn and apply Christ's ways to her life realizes *the principle of sowing and reaping applies to everyone . . . even me.* As Christians, we may look around and see beautiful crops in our lives. And we are overwhelmed with gratitude toward God because we know that if He had not saved us, disciplined us, and withheld our sinful pursuits by His grace at work in our life, then our fields would have been a complete mess. Nevertheless, there are some patches of bad crops, and we realize that those were areas of our life where we were lazy and negligent.

For some people, this experience can be startling because they never took the principle of reaping and sowing seriously. And while this is hard to face, I call this a midlife grace because we get an early wake up call, a sober reminder at the midpoint of our journey that the principle of sowing and reaping applies to us all. And this is important because there is a day coming when we will give an account for the deeds done in the body, whether good or evil. But we are given time now to repent where we need to and make radical changes to live even more devoted lives for the King and His kingdom!

God has given us abundant motivation to fire us up to become women who pursue lives marked by the kingdom of God. He wants us to become sowers and reapers of kingdom crops, which have present and future benefits for our lives and that bless others. If the judgment seat has its proper work in our lives, then we will replace laziness with liveliness for the kingdom of God. Dormant gifts will be awakened and used in powerful ways. Gifts that are already being used will become more refined. And new adventures with the King will be launched.

If the judgment seat has its proper work in our lives, then we will replace laziness with liveliness for the kingdom of God.

For example, I know a woman who struggled with financial stewardship. But when she began to meditate on the judgment seat of Christ, she was motivated to use her resources for the kingdom of God. As she began to seek Him for guidance, a new passion arose in her heart to support a missionary and his family. She found herself becoming strangely excited to send money to such a significant cause and wondered why she hadn't lived this way before.

One day when the missionary was back in the States, he visited her family to tell them about the glorious gospel works he had seen. While the woman's children were listening, they were inspired to begin serving the Lord themselves!

If the judgment seat of Christ has its proper effect on our lives, new love and zeal will begin propelling us into further kingdom living. The result? More love, more joy, and, as hard as it is to believe, more eternal rewards!

REPLACING LAZINESS WITH LIVELINESS

Let's consider how to enjoy God more now by becoming like Him and participating in His kingdom business, which will result in more eternal joy.

1. How does the biblical teaching of the judgment seat of Christ and eternal rewards motivate you to grow in your obedience in faith and to serve the King with excellence and diligence?

2. What are some remaining sin patterns in your life? For example, perhaps you struggle with something like anger and have settled into this sinful pattern, thinking "this is just the way I am." Take time to meditate on 2 Corinthians 5:9–10. Consider that you will give an account for every time you "rage" on your spouse, children, or coworkers (Eph. 4:31 NIV). How does the judgment seat of Christ motivate you to turn that intensity toward growing out of sin and replacing it with the kindness and tenderheartedness of Christ (Eph. 4:26, 31–32)?

3. One way to grow out of laziness into spiritual fervor is to make a schedule for devotional time with Christ. Start meditating on the beatitudes in Matthew 5–7. Mentally gaze on the beautiful character of your King and begin applying His good ways to your life. He has a lot to teach us about what we allow to roll around in our mind (e.g., lust), how to love and forgive others, how to handle our anger, money, and more. Take time to savor the present day rewards of participating in the divine life now.

4. Another way to grow in the obedience of faith is to sit down with your husband if you are married and begin talking about changes you can make as a family to live more for the King and His kingdom. Perhaps the two of you need to become more diligent in stewarding your time, gifts, or finances for the kingdom. Perhaps you could discuss together how to free each other up from trivial things and support the other's gifts and callings.

5. Sometimes people look at spiritual gifts as "fun things" to know about ourselves and to use at leisure. Have you ever considered that you will give an account for how diligent you are with your gifts and engaging in kingdom business? Take time to begin discovering the gifts God has given you and how you can begin using them for His kingdom in a way that fits with the current season of life He has you in.

6. Is God calling you to remain righteous while suffering under a harsh boss or other forms of persecution? Read 1 Peter 2:18–20; 3:9. How are you motivated to resist retaliating and continue trusting in God by looking forward to the rewards of the righteous?

7. Is God calling you to make radical sacrifices in your life right now? If yes, read Luke 2:18–30. How does it motivate you to keep obeying Christ by faith to know that He will richly reward every sacrifice you make in this life and the Age to Come?

8. If you ever start to feel overwhelmed, I would like to suggest that you pause and do what a dear friend often counsels me to do: "Just do the next right thing." You will not achieve perfect obedience in this life. But you can grow by doing the next right thing, step by step.

CHAPTER 11

WALKING THROUGH THE CITY OF GOD

*Walk about Zion and go around her; count her towers;
consider her ramparts; go through her palaces, that you may
tell it to the next generation.*

—Psalm 48:12–13 NASB

When people think about the Age to Come, they often envision a cloudy, disembodied state. This is often a disturbing image to people because we love the earth and the tangible things it contains.

My daughter and I like to take off our shoes in the summer and walk on a warm dirt road that leads to the lake; we like sitting on big rocks at sunset as our unbound hair flows freely in the wind; and we enjoy eating strawberries while lying on soft green grass.

On a slightly more sophisticated level, my friends and I delight in drinking coffee together at outdoor bistros and walking through boutiques where we "ooh" and "aah" over fragrant candles. And I love picking out a cute dress for date nights with my husband in downtown Houston.

Why do we like these kinds of things? We are earthy people. We have a connection to the material world because God made humanity from the dust of the earth to live on it (Gen. 2:7). We enjoy the world God created and the beauties that come from it. But this is not the whole of us.

We are also spiritual people. After God made man from the earth, He breathed into his nostrils the breath of life and set eternity into our hearts (Gen. 2:7; Eccl. 3:11). And so we see that God has made us unique! Though we are earthy people, we will be the most miserable of people if we live as materialists who think the world is all there is, because our hearts are made for God and eternity. We are physical and spiritual beings. And a prominent theme in the Bible is that God is going to create a physical place where He will live in the midst of His people, providing spiritual and material blessings forever.

Notice the glorious cluster of psalms that point forward to the coming King and His worldwide kingdom. Though these psalms were inspired by specific occasions for the day in which they were written, they also have a higher fulfillment with Jesus Christ in view. Psalm 45 points forward to the coming King and His bride. Psalm 46 points forward to the climactic day of the Lord. Then follows Psalm 47, which exhorts us to shout with loud joy and celebration as our victorious warrior King takes His universal

throne and manifests His reign throughout
the world. Then Psalm 48 celebrates the
beauty and glory of Zion, the City of our
great King!

LET'S TAKE A WALKABOUT!

In Psalm 48, the Holy Spirit calls us to join the psalmist in meditating on the presence of God in Zion. And He tells us to do that
in a specific way; namely, by considering His lovingkindness to
dwell with His people, resulting in a strong and beautiful city,
which will be "the joy of the whole earth" (v. 2 NASB):

> We have *thought on Your lovingkindness*, O God, in
> the midst of Your temple. As is Your name, O God,
> so is Your praise to the ends of the earth; Your right hand
> is full of righteousness. Let Mount Zion be glad, let the
> daughters of Judah rejoice because of Your judgments. (vv.
> 9–11 NASB)

After calling us to meditate on God's lovingkindness in view
of His glorious city, the psalmist goes on to say that as God's
reputation and fame reaches to the end of the earth, so will His
praise! As we have seen, every glorious feature of the Age to
Come will cause us to become a society of praise for our King.
And now we see this truth once again as we are invited to celebrate God by considering His strong and majestic city where He
will protect and provide for His people forever.

In verses 12–13a the Holy Spirit tells us to "Walk about Zion and go around her; count her towers; consider her ramparts; go through her palaces." Why does God want us to walk through, examine, inspect, and consider with our minds the magnificent city of God? He goes on to answer: "that you may tell *it* to the next generation. For such is God, our God forever and ever; He will guide us until death" (vv. 13b–14 NASB).

How thrilling! As we consider the safe, beautiful, and joyful place where God will dwell in the midst of His people, our hearts will be led to marvel at His lovingkindness toward us, and we will be moved to tell others about God and His city so that they too will put their hope in Him. So let's take a walk through the city of God, and then we will consider some specific ways it will motivate us to pursue lives marked by the kingdom of God.

DAVID. DEVOTION. DWELLING.

You may laugh when I tell you that we are going to launch our walkabout from God's promise to David in 2 Samuel 7 that we looked at in chapter 8. There are so many treasures in this chest! But this time, we will consider God's promise to David through Psalm 132, which is a reflection on 2 Samuel 7. The psalm begins by focusing on David's love and devotion for God, which led David to ask God if he could build a dwelling place for Him. David said,

> "I will not enter my house or get into my bed, I will not give sleep to my eyes or slumber to my eyelids, until I find a place for the LORD, a dwelling place for the Mighty One of Jacob." (vv. 3–5)

David wants to build a dwelling place or temple for God in the capital city of Jerusalem, which is also called Zion. He said he would not even be comfortable in his own palace until he found a place for God. As you know by now, God responded by saying that David was not the one who would build God a dwelling place. But God had something far better in mind. God will make His dwelling with David's descendants and Christ's people forever (Rev. 21:2–3). Implicit in God's oath to David was that God will dwell with David and His people in Zion, the city where God will abundantly bless His people spiritually and materially forever.[1] Psalm 132 goes on to say:

> The LORD swore to David a sure oath from which he will not turn back: "One of the sons of your body I will set on your throne. If your sons keep my covenant and my testimonies that I shall teach them, their sons also forever shall sit on your throne."
>
> For the LORD has chosen Zion; he has desired it for his dwelling place: "This is my resting place forever; here I will dwell, for I have desired it. I will abundantly bless her provisions; I will satisfy her poor with bread. Her priests I will clothe with salvation, and her saints will shout for joy. There I will make a horn to sprout for David; I have prepared a lamp for my anointed. His enemies I will clothe with shame, but on him his crown will shine." (vv. 11–18)

I love how God's promise to build a place for David and his descendants to dwell with Him was birthed out of their love and devotion to one another! Of course, God's dwelling with His people is at the heart of the biblical message, and it extends far beyond David to God's original design for creation as seen in Eden. But God moved His plan forward through His sacred relationship with David.

The reason I've launched our walkabout through the majestic city of God from Psalm 132 is because I want us to marvel together that the most glorious feature of the city of God is that it will be the place where God will dwell with us forever. This is highlighted through David's devotion and desire to dwell with God, as well as, God's stunning promise in response. And as we are about to see, the ultimate fulfillment of this promise will take place when Jesus reigns from the city of God in the Age to Come.[2]

THE FUTURE METROPOLIS OF THE WORLD

The city of God is described with rich imagery in Isaiah 60. When Jesus returns to manifest His reign throughout the world, we will see Jerusalem (Zion) become the glorious metropolis of the world where everyone will want to be:

> Arise, shine, for your light has come, and the glory of the LORD has risen upon you. For behold, darkness shall cover the earth, and thick darkness the peoples; but the LORD will arise upon you, and his glory will be seen upon you. And nations shall come to your light, and kings to the brightness of your rising.
>
> Lift up your eyes all around, and see; they all gather together, they come to you; your sons shall come from afar, and your daughters shall be carried on the hip. (vv. 1–4)

After our warrior King executes judgment, thick darkness will cover the earth. But from the darkness will arise a beautiful and attractive light over Zion. And the light will be the glory of the Lord! Jesus will enter into the city that He has chosen to be His dwelling place. And *believers* from all nations will come streaming to Christ's bright and beautiful light.

And what will we see when we arrive? The Holy Spirit goes on to describe the city as a place of abundant material wealth.

A City of Abundant Wealth and Security

Then you shall see and be radiant; your heart shall thrill and exult, because the abundance of the sea shall be turned to you, the wealth of the nations shall come to you. (Isa. 60:5)

It is incredible to consider how God has created all kinds of glorious materials, such as gold, diamonds, and more, and put them in different places of the earth for humanity to discover and excavate. Fallen humanity has often used these beautiful and luxurious resources to build things for our own sinful pleasures. But on that day, the nations will bring their riches to the city of God out of heartfelt worship for Him. And with these materials, God says, "I will beautify my beautiful house" (v. 7).

The gates to God's majestic metropolis will also be open continually. It is hard to imagine the security we will experience in the Age to Come under Christ's rule. The gates to the city will be open at all times. And don't miss this: the reason the gates are left open is so that people can continue to bring their wealth (v. 11). In other words, not only will there be no fear of people taking possessions, but the gates are open so people can continue to bring in the wealth of the nations to God's majestic city!

It is thrilling to meditate on the city of God, where life will be filled with such peace and security that the gates will be open continually.

My husband's family is from the Philippines, where they own beach-front property on which they farm coconuts, mangos, and fish—definitely my kind of farm. Many members of his family have dual citizenship with the United States, which enables them to travel back and forth during different seasons.

One day I was talking with Bobby's cousin, and I made the comment that the Philippines would be a beautiful place to return to for missions in their retirement years. But her response was surprising. She said that most of her family would probably choose to remain in the United States rather than return to their beachfront property because rebels have grown in power and often threaten to kill and steal from landowners.

Sadly, this is a common story for many people throughout the world. I have a friend from Central America who fled from her beautiful country to find refuge in another because of the ruthless violence of powerful gangs in her land. In view of these frightening realities in our fallen world, it is thrilling to meditate on the city of God, where life will be filled with such peace and security that the gates will be open continually. And it is worth slowing down to note that the reason it will be such a safe city is because Jesus Christ, the King who loves righteousness and hates wickedness, will be ruling from there!

Solomon's golden age was a preview of the prosperity of Christ's kingdom. But due to Israel's idolatry, God exiled the nation. As a result, Jerusalem has been known as a city forsaken and despised (Isa. 60:14–15). But God will restore her fortunes. As a nursing child gets sustenance from its mother's milk, Jerusalem will be sustained by the wealth of the nations (vv. 11, 16). God will make Jerusalem majestic forever (v. 15). When we see this stunning turn of fortunes, we will "know that I, the LORD, am your Savior and your Redeemer, the Mighty One of Jacob" (v. 16). He will make the city of God a joy from age to age, the famous metropolis of the world, the place where everyone will want to be!

A City of Righteousness, Peace, and Joy

What else will we see in the city of God? Isaiah 60, in verses 17–22, goes on to describe the city as a place that will be filled with righteous people, peace, and joy. All Zion's citizens will be righteous, displaying the moral splendor of God. In fact, consider this stunning statement: "I will make your overseers peace and *your taskmasters righteousness.* Violence shall no more be heard in your land, devastation or destruction within your borders; you shall call your walls Salvation, and your gates Praise" (vv. 17b–18).

In this fallen age, our sin nature is like a taskmaster over us. My daughter was recently trying to fight a temptation and said, "Mommy, my heart is *begging* me to sin." I was amazed at how clearly she articulated the human experience of sin! Sin rigorously drives, burdens, and begs us to throw off God's good limits and go our own way. This may be one of the most thrilling aspects of God's city to me. Righteousness will inspire and compel us to love God's moral beauty and do good to one another!

We can get lost in many sweet meditations of what it will be like to live in a society of people who reflect the moral goodness of God—His righteousness. One meditation that leads me into eager anticipation for the Age to Come is to consider what it will be like when redeemed humanity produces art and music. Can you imagine walking through an art gallery in the city of God, where the good and beautiful features of humanity according to God's design are put on display? Or consider walking with your friends through the city and hearing beautiful music that sweeps you up in awe of God and love, kindness, and fellowship with others.

Righteousness will be everywhere, resulting in a society of peace and joy. And what will be the result? Here it is again: when we walk through the city of God, which is filled with wealth, security, peace, righteousness, and joy, we will sing the praise of the One who built it: the "people shall all be righteous; they shall possess the land forever, the branch of my [God's] planting, the work of my hands, that I [God] might be glorified" (v. 21).

A Majestic Home Forever

Forever is a magnificent word! Believers will not be sojourners forever. Missionaries will not be on the move forever. Believing refugees will not be cast out and homeless forever. Believing immigrants will not be without citizenship in a great country forever. Tight budgets will not be forever. Trying to be wise and save money for old age when our strength is gone will not be forever. Facing disease and physical death will not be forever.

Living with God in the majestic city of God *will* be forever!

Thus, Hebrews 11 teaches us to imitate the faith of Abraham by being ready to follow God even if it means leaving our homes or lands, knowing we are citizens of an everlasting city. When God called Abraham to leave his home and go to the place he would later receive as an inheritance, Abraham believed God and obeyed Him (Gen. 12:1; Heb. 11:8). And we are told that Abraham's faith and obedience was fueled by God's promise. Abraham was "looking forward to the city that has foundations, whose designer and builder is God" (Heb. 11:10).

Many of us do desire to take kingdom adventures with God, but there can be a point when the uprooting and moving can become tiresome and, as scary as this sounds, we may even find ourselves becoming closed off to the idea of following God into new kingdom ventures. Or perhaps we struggle with following God when He calls because we love the place where God currently has us—whether it is our home, city, local church, or place of work. But Jesus does graciously interrupt our lives and may even call us to follow Him to a new place for the sake of the gospel. It is during these times that meditating on the city of God will provide worship and fuel for obedience.

There was a particular season of my life when God called Bobby and me to be on the move for specific kingdom works at a more intense level than usual. We moved three times in three years. Our first move was a step of faith, because God called us to sell our beautiful home in a lake community north of Houston to move into an apartment in the city so we could be close to the church where we would be serving. It was hard to give away a lot of our possessions in order to downsize, but we adjusted quickly due to the joy of ministry in the city.

However, right when we seemed to be adjusting, God called Bobby to Louisville, Kentucky, for one year to finish his seminary degree. I will never forget the phone call when Bobby announced the news to me. I happened to be on the phone with the women's ministry leader of a large church in Houston who had invited me to speak at their summer event when Bobby's call beeped in. When I called him back, he shared with me that he believed God was calling us to go to Louisville. My heart dropped from surprise and disappointment. My ministry and friendships were flourishing in the city that I love. I had no desire to go elsewhere.

Right when Bobby announced the news to me, a tweet came through on my phone from a pastor talking about the beauty of submission! I knew it was not a coincidence. I grabbed my Bible to seek God and opened to Proverbs 11:23: "The desire of the righteous ends only in good." It seemed that God was reminding me that He knows the desires of my heart and that I will never be disappointed in the end when I follow Him. All these things happened within ten minutes, affirming God's leadership through my husband.

Since Bobby would be attending school fulltime, we would have to be on a tighter budget. So we began looking for an inexpensive place to live. Everything we attempted to secure continued to fall through until finally one place worked out. We packed our bags and headed to Louisville. When we drew near to our new dwelling place, the navigator began leading us up a winding hill that was lined on both sides with lush green trees that created an archway over the road. The beautiful view caused me to warm up a bit to the new adventure set before us, and I thought, *This is kind of enchanting.*

But when we got to the top of the hill, it was like the record scratched at a party just when everyone was starting to have a good time. People were sitting on lawn chairs in front of their townhomes, violent music was echoing throughout the streets, herds of young kids were playing in the street without supervision, and grown men loudly cussed at one another. Bobby and I laugh now looking back at that day because he didn't even look at me—he knew full well what I was thinking. These things were not featured on the website!

Though there was some discussion about whether or not we should try to get out of our lease, we both knew at the end of the day that this was the dwelling place God had chosen for us. We had prayed for months while looking at various places online from Houston, and everything continued to get thwarted, except this one little treasure—a little city on a hill. And so we decided to stay and trust that God had put us there to share Christ with the people in the neighborhood. We took steps to be wise by purchasing extra locks for the door and other safety measures and set out to love the people in the neighborhood.

One day Jade and I were outside with three neighborhood boys. While playing together, Jade began telling the boys about Jesus and the gospel. And as I looked into a little boy's eyes while he drank in the gospel from the mouth of my daughter—whose Rs still sounded the Ws when she said, "Jesus died, and He 'wose' again, and He will never die again"—my eyes filled with tears as I thought, *This is far more beautiful than granite countertops.* It had been hard to leave my home—and then leave the city and church that I love—to follow Christ to new places. But in that moment I was so grateful to be part of His grand mission to tell these children about Christ and perhaps lead some of them into the kingdom.

Born Free Citizens

I encourage you to read Psalm 87, which is about Zion and those who are blessed to be its citizens. Birthright language is all over this psalm: "And of Zion it shall be said, 'This one and that one were born in her'; for the Most High himself will establish her. The LORD records as he registers the peoples, 'This one was born there'" (vv. 5–6).

Let's think about birthright citizenship. In some countries, a child is granted citizenship when they are born within the jurisdiction of that country, if not within the natural borders of the country itself. For example, a child born in the US Virgin Islands is granted United States citizenship.

In a similar way, Psalm 87 points forward to the new spiritual birth that Jesus talks about in John 3:3–8 and the citizenship God grants to His children. When someone is spiritually born again by grace through faith in Jesus Christ, they are given citizenship in the city of God (Luke 10:20; Phil. 3:20). God is pictured as entering the new birth on Zion's registry in heaven. It does not matter where these people are born or where they are citizens in this age; they can become citizens of the city of God!

And while we will not physically step into the city of God until the Age to Come, Hebrews 12:22–24 says that new covenant believers have been granted access to God, we have already begun heavenly activities, and have been brought into a heavenly society and fellowship now:

> You [believers in Jesus Christ] have come to Mount Zion and to the city of the living God, the heavenly Jerusalem, and to innumerable angels in festal gathering, and to the assembly of the firstborn who are enrolled in heaven, and to God, the judge of all, and to the spirits of the righteous made perfect, and to Jesus, the mediator of a new covenant, and to the sprinkled blood that speaks a better word than the blood of Abel. (Heb. 12:22–24)

It is thrilling to consider who the citizens of this city are: Jesus Christ our Mediator, whose blood made it possible for us to enter into His city; Old Testament believers; innumerable angels in festive gathering; and the church of the firstborn, a title that exalts Jesus as having supreme honor and position in our new family, while also communicating the staggering news that believers have been made fellow heirs with Christ—people who will inherit the world and rule with Him. We have already been brought into fellowship with this great cloud of witnesses (Heb. 12:1), these citizens of God's city through the Holy Spirit.

We get little tastes of the kingdom all the time. And while we might be able to experience some of these things spiritually, we are not there yet physically. Our bodies will continue to break down and die. But Christians can handle these struggles differently than unbelievers because we know where we are going. So like Abraham, Moses, and everyone else in Hebrews 11, we are looking ahead to when our bodies catch up with our hearts at God's mountain!

SEEKING A BETTER COUNTRY

1. Read Hebrews 11:13–14. The heroes of faith who have gone before us acknowledged that God's promises would not be consummated in this world. Therefore, they did not try to build castles for themselves here. Instead, they "acknowledged that they were strangers and exiles on the earth" (v. 13). And talking like that made it "clear that they are seeking a country of their own" (v. 14 NASB). Are you trying to build your castle here, or do you live in a way that demonstrates that you are living for your true home in a better country? What changes can you make to demonstrate your faith of seeking and desiring God's country by living more for the gospel now?

2. Jesus calls some people to give up their home to follow Him to new places for gospel ministry. Please read Luke 9:57–59 and Luke 18:18–30. How do these verses, as well as Hebrews 11:13–14, motivate you to be ready to follow Christ, even if it means giving up your home?

3. After talking about the access we have been given to the heavenly city in Hebrews 12:22–24, Hebrews 13 gives us practical ways to live as exiles on this earth. Please read this chapter. Hebrews 13:2 tells us to be hospitable. How does your citizenship in the city of God motivate you to show hospitality?

4. Hebrews 13:5–6 says, "Keep your life free from love of money, and be content with what you have, for he [Jesus] has said, 'I will never leave you nor forsake you.' So we can confidently

say, 'The Lord is my helper; I will not fear; what can man do to me?'" Relying on Jesus' promise to help you, what are some areas in which you would like to be set free from the love of money and the pursuit of your castles in this life?

5. Hebrews 13:16 tells us not to neglect sharing our spiritual and material blessings with others. God is generous and will share His city with us! What are some specific ways that God's generous nature and your citizenship in the city of God inspire you to be more generous?

CHAPTER 12

COURAGE, DEAR HEART

*Has this world been so kind to you that you should
leave it with regret? There are better things ahead than any
we leave behind.*[1]

—C. S. Lewis

Readers of C. S. Lewis's The Chronicles of Narnia series will recognize the title of this chapter as words spoken by Aslan, the lion who is the Christ figure.[2] Aslan is bolstering the courage of young Lucy, who was in the midst of a great adventure.

The Christian life is far from a humdrum experience. It is an epic adventure that involves decisions that determine our destiny, a journey that requires courage.

It takes courage to leave behind our self-made ventures and take the adventure of new life with Christ. It takes courage to grow up and become who we are—namely, representatives of the King who share the good news of His kingdom in a world that is in opposition to Him. It takes courage to fight seductive temptations that lead us astray. It takes courage to not pack up our sail and turn in for an early night or to take a last few big gulps of idolatrous loves when we face mortality at midlife. And it takes courage to face death.

Where does courage come from? It comes from trusting God and His promises to be with us to the end of the Age, to deliver us from death itself, and to bring us into the destiny we have longed for all of our lives:

> Therefore do not throw away your confidence, which has a great reward. For you have need of endurance, so that when you have done the will of God you may receive what is promised. For, "Yet a little while, and the coming one will come and will not delay; but my righteous one shall live by faith, and if he shrinks back, my soul has no pleasure in him." But we are not of those who shrink back and are destroyed, but of those who have faith and preserve their souls. . . . Now faith is the assurance of things hoped for, the conviction of things not seen . . . And without faith it is impossible to please him [God], for whoever would draw near to God must believe that he exists and that he rewards those who seek him. (Heb. 10:35–39; 11:1, 6)

We are in this together! Let's help one another to not throw away our confidence. Let's take what we have learned and continue to cultivate our all-consuming goal to please God by setting our minds on the glorious reward in Christ, which will be given to those who persevere in God's will. Let's fire up our faith that produces endurance by continuing to set our minds on the staggering glories to come and pursuing lives marked by the kingdom of God.

COURAGE FOR YOUNG WOMEN

If you are a young woman finishing this book, I am praying for you to have courage to take the adventure of new life with Christ. Once you are spiritually born again, it will take courage and tenacity to stay awake to reality, and you can do this by continuing to set your mind on the vivid pictures of what-is and what-is-to-come. May your faith be rewarded in this age by growing in the wonder of knowing your King and being His bride. May you become steadfast and effective in representing your Bridegroom in this present age. And may you experience the reward of becoming more like Christ each day, knowing you are also storing up rich rewards in the Age to Come.

COURAGE FOR MIDLIFE

If you are a midlifer reading this book, I am with you! God called me to begin thinking and writing about the Age to Come when I was entering into midlife. Tasting my mortality has been a sobering experience. Sadly, I have seen people in this stage of life respond to this new awareness in destructive ways. But our King is a good Shepherd who knows the perplexities of the seasons we are walking into, even when we do not have a clue.

I am thankful that our good Shepherd called me to set my mind on the glories to come precisely at the time when I began to taste my mortality at a new level. By doing so, He has helped me maintain a bright perspective for today by setting my eyes on the eternal day of tomorrow. He has pulled me back from temptation. And He has imparted a desire to be more devoted in my kingdom adventures with Him in however many days I have left. Thus, I have experienced firsthand, once again, that God's wisdom works; and following His wisdom is not just a good suggestion—it is necessary.

There are many earthly images set before us that Satan uses to entice us away from God. I recently saw a preview of a movie about a middle-aged woman who is separated from her husband. She finds new excitement by hooking up with a young man, who then moves into her mansion with two of his young friends. When she is unsure about the living arrangement, her own mother encourages her to see it as new adventure. Moviegoers who feel exhausted, hopeless, and disinterested in life are invited to find comfort in this fantasy.

In Satan's typical way, all the themes of truth are set forth in this particular film—adventure, romantic love, and mansions— but the truth is perverted. And these perversions of the truth lead women away from God and the true adventure with Him. Satan entices women at midlife to find comfort for their souls by lingering in fantasies, which will no doubt be influential in what women begin to seek.

As I watched the preview, my heart sank with sadness for men and women who are being led astray by deceitful images such as these. Thus, it is my prayer for you and the women in our generation that we will set our minds on the glories to come, which will keep us awake to reality, where God is alive and glorious and calls us to take even more kingdom adventures with Him in this life until we return to our true home.

COURAGE TO FACE DEATH

Lastly, if you or someone you love is facing death, I pray that God will empower you with hope and courage to walk through one of life's hardest trials. God has called me to say goodbye to a precious family member and friend who died during the season that I wrote this book. And I have also had to walk through the gut-wrenching experience of learning that someone my age—who is most dear to my heart—has been diagnosed with a disease. But God has strengthened me to walk through these hard realities and to encourage others with the vivid truths we have discussed throughout this book.

C. S. Lewis corresponded with a sick and dying friend named Mary on June 17, 1963. A doctor had refused to treat her, and she was facing death. Lewis wrote these words to her:

> Pain is terrible, but surely you need not have fear as well? Can you not see death as the friend and deliverer? It means stripping off that body which is tormenting you: like taking off a hair-shirt or getting out of a dungeon. What is there to be afraid of? You have long attempted (and none of us does more) a Christian life. Your sins are confessed and absolved. Has this world been so kind to you that you should leave it with regret? There are better things ahead than any we leave behind.[3]

May God grant us courage and endurance to face death together as a passageway to the destiny we have always longed for by keeping our faith fired up for Christ and the better things ahead.

"Now to him who is able to keep you from stumbling and to present you blameless before the presence of his glory with great joy, to the only God, our Savior, through Jesus Christ our Lord, be glory, majesty, dominion, and authority, before all time and now and forever. Amen." (Jude 24–25)

And amen.

NOTES

Chapter 1: Longing for the Age to Come

1. G. K. Chesterton, *Orthodoxy,* Moody Classics (Chicago: Moody, 2009), 83. Chesterton lived in a time of tremendous scientific discoveries, when we started to understand the world around us in ways no one had before. As a result, many people moved toward *materialism* and *naturalism.* That is, some people thought they had come to understand the laws of nature and that, as a result, they couldn't be surprised anymore. For example, a materialist or naturalist may conclude that since people do not die and come back to life again, it could never happen. Chesterton cautioned against this, talking about how people in his day could understand the world more and more but could not understand themselves. They have "forgotten their name" because they have lost the ability to be surprised and to wonder. Chesterton's point is that we have to be careful not to think we have everything figured out; we have to remain open to God doing something new. See Quentin Lauer, *G. K. Chesterton: Philosopher Without Portfolio* (New York: Fordham University Press, 2004), 97; G. K. Chesterton, *G. K. Chesterton: The Dover Reader* (Mineola, NY: Dover Publications, 2014), 291–93.

2. Scripture is clear that we were created to live in an intimate relationship with the King of kings and uses many metaphors to describe this truth. "For the LORD Most High is awesome, the great King over all the earth" (Ps. 47:2 NIV). When God created humanity, He made us in His image to know Him and to thrive in submission to His good rule over our lives. God often describes our relationship with Him using the most intimate metaphor known to man—namely, marriage (Hos. 1–3; Eph. 5:22–33; Rev. 19:6–9). God created us to experience the fullness of joy in His glorious presence, which is sometimes described in Scripture as a kind of marital joy between a bride and her bridegroom (Isa. 62:4–5). We are made to love God above all things, live in joyful submission to Him, and desire to please Him (Luke 10:27; 2 Cor. 3:18).

3. John Calvin, *Commentaries on the Book of Genesis,* vol. 1, Calvin's Commentaries, trans. Rev. John King (Grand Rapids: Baker, 1993), 227–28.

4. Steve Corbett and Brian Fikkert, *When Helping Hurts* (Chicago: Moody,

2012), 62–63. Corbett and Fikkert talk about four types of poverty that are effects from the fall: poverty of spiritual intimacy, poverty of being, poverty of community, and poverty of stewardship.

5. George Eldon Ladd, *A Theology of the New Testament,* rev. ed. (Grand Rapids: Eerdmans, 1974), 44–45.

6. C. S. Lewis, *Surprised by Joy* (London: Harcourt, 1955), 238.

7. I am indebted to John Piper for helping me understand how rewards such as cities and crowns in the Age to Come can be received in a way that do not compete with God but enhance our joy in Him. Desiringgod.org includes an ongoing collection of many of Piper's interviews, messages, and sermons collected in a wide body of work and presented over more than two decades. See interview "What is the Appeal of Heavenly Rewards Other Than Getting Christ?" March 27, 2017: http://www.desiringgod.org/interviews/what-s-the-appeal-of-heavenly-rewards-other-than-getting-christ.

8. G. K. Chesterton, *G.K. Chesterton: The Dover Reader* (Mineola, NY: Dover Publications, 2014), 296. Chesterton explains the concept of "fairy-tale philosopher" in contrast with his context of nineteenth-century determinism and scientific realism. For example, people say that fairy tales are for children. When we grow up, and practical life takes over, then we discover the truth. But Chesterton says his experience of coming to the truth was the opposite. There are some shadows of truth in fairy tales that he learned as a child that point to what is really happening in the universal story of life.

Chapter 2: Powerful Pictures of the Age to Come

1. Lucy says this in C. S. Lewis, *The Lion, the Witch, and the Wardrobe* (New York: HarperCollins, 1994). It was also the tagline for the 2005 film adaptation (Walt Disney Company and Walden Media).

2. This is what the Bible says about itself: "All Scripture is breathed out by God" (inspiration, 2 Tim. 3:16). Since Scripture comes from God, who is perfect, the Word of God is without error in its original writings (inerrancy, Prov. 30:5, Ps. 18:30). And because the Word of God is perfect, everything that it says has happened, is happening now, or will happen in the future is true (infallibility, Ps. 19:7). And so we see that the Word of God is inspired, inerrant, and infallible; therefore, it is all we need for life and godliness. In other words, it is sufficient (sufficiency, 2 Peter 1:3–4, 2 Tim. 3:17).

3. Leland Ryken, *How to Read the Bible as Literature* (Grand Rapids: Zondervan, 1984), 167, 174.

4. Jerry Fine and Marilyn Fine, *One on One with God* (Enumclaw, WA: Winepress, 2003); also used by the authors in unpublished form as a teaching resource at Houston's First Baptist Church, Houston, Texas.

5. "The real labor is to remember, to attend [to the presence of God]. In fact, to come awake. Still more, to remain awake." C. S. Lewis, *Letters to Malcolm* (London: Geoffrey Bles, 1964), 75.

6. C. S. Lewis, letter to Mary Willis Shelburne, June 28, 1963, in *The Collected Letters of C. S. Lewis,* vol. 3: *Narnia, Cambridge, and Joy, 1950–1963,* ed. Walter Hooper (San Francisco: HarperSanFrancisco, 2007), 1,434; quoted in Kevin J. Vanhoozer, "In Bright Shadow: C. S. Lewis on the Imagination for Theology and Discipleship," in *The Romantic Rationalist: God, Life, and Imagination in the Work of C. S. Lewis,* eds. John Piper and David Mathis (Wheaton, IL: Crossway, 2014), 82–83.

7. Vanhoozer talks about what is and what will be in Christ, "In Bright Shadow: C. S. Lewis on the Imagination for Theology and Discipleship," in *The Romantic Rationalist: God, Life, and Imagination in the Work of C. S. Lewis,* eds. John Piper and David Mathis (Wheaton, IL: Crossway, 2014), 82–83.

8. Jerry Fine and Marilyn Fine, *One on One with God.*

Chapter 3: The Supreme Adventure of Life

1. G. K. Chesterton, *Orthodoxy*, Moody Classics (Chicago: Moody, 2009), 20–22.

2. Chesterton said "an adventure is only an inconvenience rightly considered. An inconvenience is only an adventure wrongly considered." G. K. Chesterton, "On Running after One's Hat," in *All Things Considered* (New York: Sheed & Ward, 1955), 28, quoted in G. K. Chesterton, *The Collected Works of G. K. Chesterton,* vol. 7 (San Francisco: Ignatius Press, 2005), 17.

3. Chesterton, *Orthodoxy*, 76–83. Chesterton uses this language to describe the world of wonder in fairy tales and indirectly points to the content of the Christian faith. He thinks fairy tales written by common man contain some commonsense truths, which Christianity affirms. Rationalism is a worldview where everything is explainable through science and the material universe. This worldview holds that there is no Creator or intentional design for it. Thus, rationalism does not elicit wonder and praise from us. But Christianity says creation is made by a Creator who wants us to see His wonder through it. Thus, Chesterton argues that in some ways, fairy tales help us see the world of wonder better than the fallen worldviews of men.

4. D. A. Carson, "Christ Reigns over All: Biblical Survey of God's King-dom," interview (Desiring God Ministries, January 20, 2017), http://www.desiringgod.org/interviews/christ-reigns-over-all-biblical-survey-of-god-s-kingdom.

5. Stephen G. Dempster, *Dominion and Dynasty* (Downers Grove, IL: InterVarsity Press, 2003), 59. I am indebted to Dempster for helping me to see the biblical story of dominion and dynasty.

6. To see the idea of blessings and limits, see Chesterton, *Orthodoxy*, 84–88.

7. Ibid., 216.

Chapter 4: Taking the Adventure

1. For example, we surrendered dominion to Satan, who became the prince of the world (Eph. 2:2, Luke 4:6). Demonic thrones and prin-cipalities were set up in the heavenly realms (Eph. 6:12; Col. 2:15). Humanity became slaves to sin, Satan, and death (John 8:34; Rom. 6:6; Eph. 2:1–2; Heb. 2:14–15; 1 Cor. 15:55–57). And creation was sub-jected to futility (Rom. 8:20). We did not lose God's image on us after the fall, but as the rest of Scripture reveals, God's image became greatly deformed on us (Gen. 9:6; Rom. 3:10–12, 5:12, 15).

2. Stephen G. Dempster, *Dominion and Dynasty* (Downers Grove, IL; InterVarsity Press, 2003), 231.

3. Ur was the land that Abraham and his ancestors were from. It was "Ur-Ba'u, king of Ur, who built the temple of the moon-god." The entire city of "Ur was consecrated to the worship of Sin, the Babylonian moon-god. Therefore, Abraham most likely was worshiping the moon when God called him." M. G. Easton, *Easton's Bible Dictionary* (Albany, OR: Thomas Nelson, 1897), 1175.

4. Dempster, *Dominion and Dynasty*, 81–82.

5. C. S. Lewis, *Letters to an American Lady*, ed. Clyde S. Kilby (Grand Rapids: Eerdmans, 1967, 2014), 124.

6. Robert D. Bergen, vol. 7, *1, 2 Samuel: An Exegetical and Theological Ex-position of Holy Scripture* (The New American Commentary) (Nashville: Broadman & Holman Publishers, 1996), 337.

7. Dempster, *Dominion and Dynasty*, 217.

Chapter 5: A King Worth Living For

1. You can see many examples of these psalms at https://www.gotques-tions.org/Psalms-Jesus-Christ.html.

2. The Hebrew Bible certainly provides many analogies of the relation-ship between God and the Israelites as that of husband and wife (see

Hos. 1–3; Jer. 2; Ezek. 16, 23; Isa. 62:1–5). The Christian Scriptures continue the analogy (see Matt. 9:15; John 3:29; Eph. 5:22–23; Rev. 19:7–9). Nancy deClaisse-Walford, Rolf A. Jacobson, and Beth LaNeel Tanner, *The Book of Psalms* (Grand Rapids: Eerdmans, 2014), 417.

3. William S. Plumer, *Psalms: A Critical and Expository Commentary with Doctrinal and Practical Remarks,* Geneva Series of Commentaries (Carlisle, PA: Banner of Truth Trust, 1867, reprinted 2016), 16–18.

4. C. S. Lewis, *Reflections on the Psalms* (New York: Harcourt, Brace, 1958), 101–15.

5. I learned this biblical line of reasoning from Jonathan Edwards, *Religious Affections* (Carlisle, PA: Banner of Truth Trust, 2001), 181–83.

6. The Jews of Jesus' day had attached all sorts of nationalistic ideas to the concepts of the Messiah and the kingdom of God. Jesus took the idea of the kingdom of God as it is found in the Old Testament, and He transformed it, changing it "from a narrow-minded nationalistic hope to a universal, spiritual order" where humankind "could find the fulfillment of its ultimate desires for righteousness, justice, peace, happiness, freedom from sin and guilt, and a restored relationship to God—an order in which God was king." C. C. Caragounis, "The Kingdom of God/ Heaven," in *Dictionary of Jesus and the Gospels: a Compendium of Contemporary Biblical Scholarship*, eds. Joel B. Green, Scot McKnight and I. Howard Marshall (Downers Grove, IL: InterVarsity, 1992), 429–30.

7. Chesterton, *Orthodoxy*, 50–70.

8. Jim Hamilton, "Psalm 45: 'The King's Conquest, Throne, and Bride,'" March 20, 2016: https://www.mixcloud.com/kenwoodbaptist-church/psalm-45-the-kings-conquest-throne-and-bride-jim-hamilton-3202016/.

9. Sinclair B. Ferguson, *The Holy Spirit* (Downers Grove, IL: InterVarsity Press, 1996), 48–49.

10. Kenneth S. Wuest, *Wuest's Word Studies from the Greek New Testament for the English Reader* (Grand Rapids: Eerdmans, 1997), 1 Peter 1:8.

11. William S. Plumer, *Psalms: A Critical and Expository Commentary with Doctrinal and Practical Remarks,* Geneva Series of Commentaries (Carlisle, PA: Banner of Truth Trust, 1867, repr. 2016), 520.

Chapter 6: A Queen Is Born

1. G. K. Chesterton, *Orthodoxy*, Moody Classics (Chicago: Moody, 2009), 71–99.

2. "There can be little doubt that this psalm was in the mind of John as he wrote Revelation 19:6–21. As he looked forward to the marriage of Christ, the Lamb, in heaven, he recalled how the bride clothed herself

with acts of righteousness in preparation for Him (Rev. 19:6–8). Then John described the royal groom going forth to battle in righteousness (Rev. 19:11–21). Psalm 45, then, is typological of the greater Davidic King, Jesus Christ." Allen P. Ross, "Psalms," in *The Bible Knowledge Commentary: An Exposition of the Scriptures*, ed. John F. Walvoord and Roy B. Zuck, vol. 1 (Wheaton, IL: Victor Books, 1985), 828.

3. John Piper, *This Momentary Marriage: A Parable of Permanence* (Wheaton, IL: Crossway, 2009), 127–28.

4. You can learn more about the process of beauty and becoming in my book *Adoring Christ: Beholding God's Beauty and Becoming Like Him*, which is centered on 2 Corinthians 3:18.

5. Augustine, *Confessions*, trans. R. S. Pine-Coffin (London: Penguin Books, 1961), 21.

6. Martin Luther, *On Christian Liberty*, trans. W. A. Lambert, rev. Harold J. Grimm (Minneapolis: Fortress Press, 2003), 18–21. Also see Romans 5:19, 6:6; Ephesians 1:3, 2:6; Colossians 2:12, 3:3–4; 1 Corinthians 1:30.

7. "Priorities," April 23, 1951 in *Letters of C. S. Lewis,* 238, quoted in Wayne Martindale and Jerry Root, *The Quotable Lewis* (Wheaton, IL: Tyndale House Publishers, 1989), 496.

8. John Piper, *Brothers, We Are Not Professionals: A Plea to Pastors for Radical Ministry* (Nashville: B&H, 2013), 23. See also Piper's message "How Much Does God Love This Church?" April 18, 2010, http://www.desiringgod.org/messages/how-much-does-god-love-this-church.

Chapter 7: A Down-to-Earth Woman

1. Anthony C. Thiselton, *The First Epistle to the Corinthians: A Commentary on the Greek Text*, New International Greek Testament Commentary (Grand Rapids: Eerdmans, 2000), 357–58. For more on the Corinthians' mistiming, see also D. Fee, *The First Epistle to the Corinthians* (Grand Rapids: Eerdmans, 1987), 172; Roy E. Ciampa and Brian S. Rosner, *The First Letter to the Corinthians* (Grand Rapids: Eerdmans, 2010), 625.

2. Ibid., 358.

3. Ibid., 359–60.

4. George Eldon Ladd, *A Theology of the New Testament,* rev. ed. (Grand Rapids: Eerdmans, 1974), 45.

5. Ibid., 45, 59–61.

6. The OT closes with unfinished business. The Lord made promises that were not yet fuliflled for his people and for the world. When we read the NT, we find that God's saving promises are fulfilled, and yet these promises are realized in a surprising fashion. There is an already-but-

not-yet character to the fulfillment. Hence, the kingdom is inaugurated but not consummated. Believers enjoy eternal life now, and yet they will enjoy the fullness of such life only on the day of resurrection. Understanding the tension between the inauguration and consummation of God's promises is indispensable for grasping the message of the NT." Thomas R. Schreiner, *Magnifying God in Christ: A Summary of New Testament Theology* (Grand Rapids: Baker Books, 2010), 17.

7. Ladd, *A Theology of the New Testament*, 74.

8. See John Piper's message "Is the Kingdom Present or Future?" February 4 and February 11, 1990, http://www.desiringgod.org/messages/is-the-kingdom-present-or-future.

9. Charles Colson, Foreword, Chesterton, *Orthodoxy,* Moody Classics (Chicago: Moody, 2009), 15.

10. Colson, Foreword, *Orthodoxy*, 11–12.

11. Edwin A. Blum, "John" in *The Bible Knowledge Commentary: An Exposition of the Scriptures*, ed. J. F. Walvoord and R. B. Zuck, vol. 2 (Wheaton, IL: Victor Books, 1985), 337–38.

12. Ibid.

13. Wayne A. Grudem, *Systematic Theology: An Introduction to Biblical Doctrine* (Leicester, England; Grand Rapids: InterVarsity Press; Zondervan, 2004), 630. Grudem says, "We also share in part now in the kingly reign of Christ, since we have been raised to sit with him in the heavenly places (Eph. 2:6), thus sharing to some degree in his authority over evil spiritual forces that may be arrayed against us (Eph. 6:10–18; James 4:7; 1 Peter 5:9; 1 John 4:4)."

14. Ibid., 1082–83.

15. John Piper, *Future Grace, Revised Edition: The Purifying Power of the Promises of God* (Colorado Springs: Multnomah, 2012), 325, 327. See also Piper's article "Books That Have Influenced Me the Most," November 1, 1993, http://www.desiringgod.org/articles/books-that-have-influenced-me-most.

Chapter 8: The New Dynasty

1. Isaiah 9:7; Mark 1:1; Luke 1:33; John 20:31; Acts 9:20; Hebrews 1:5.

Chapter 9: A Moral Universe Reformed

1. John A. Martin, "Isaiah," in *The Bible Knowledge Commentary: An Exposition of the Scriptures*, ed. J. F. Walvoord and R. B. Zuck, vol. 1 (Wheaton, IL: Victor Books, 1985), 1072.

2. Martin, "Isaiah," in *The Bible Knowledge Commentary*, 1072.

3. J. A. Motyer, "The Psalms," in *New Bible Commentary: 21st Century Edition*, ed. D. A. Carson et al., 4th ed. (Leicester, England; Downers Grove, IL: InterVarsity Press, 1994), 515.

Chapter 10: Loyalists Crowned

1. Matthew 16:27; Romans 14:10–12; 1 Corinthians 3:12–15; 2 Corinthians 5:10; Revelation 22:12.
2. John MacArthur, *The MacArthur Study Bible: New American Standard Bible* (Nashville: Thomas Nelson, 2006), 1739.
3. C. S. Lewis, "The World's Last Night" (orig. 1952), in *The World's Last Night and Other Essays* (New York: Harcourt Brace Jovanovich, n.d.), 93–113.
4. C. S. Lewis, "The World's Last Night," in *The Essential C.S. Lewis*, ed. Lyle W. Dorsett (New York: Simon & Schuster, 1996), 392.
5. The terms *character* and *conduct* come from George Ladd, who said the ethics of the kingdom emphasize the righteousness of the heart: "The primary emphasis is on the inner character that underlies outward conduct." George Eldon Ladd, *A Theology of the New Testament*, rev. ed. (Grand Rapids: Eerdmans, 1974).
6. MacArthur, *The MacArthur Study Bible*, 1520.
7. Paul David Tripp, *Lost in the Middle: Midlife and the Grace of God* (Wapwallopen, PA: Shepherd Press, 2004), 103–104 (Kindle edition).

Chapter 11: Walking through the City of God

1. D. A. Carson et al., eds., *New Bible Commentary: 21st Century Edition*, 4th ed. (Leicester, England; Downers Grove, IL: InterVarsity Press, 1994), 576.
2. Psalm 132:13; Ezekiel 48:35; Hebrews 12:22; Revelation 21:2–3.

Chapter 12: Courage, Dear Heart

1. C. S. Lewis, letter to Mary Willis Shelburne, June 28, 1963, in *The Collected Letters of C. S. Lewis*, vol. 3: *Narnia, Cambridge, and Joy, 1950–1963*, ed. Walter Hooper (San Francisco: HarperSanFrancisco, 2007), 1,434.
2. C. S. Lewis, *The Voyage of the Dawn Treader* (New York: HarperCollins Publishers, 1952).
3. C. S. Lewis, *Letters to an American Lady*, ed. Clyde S. Kilby (Grand Rapids: Eerdmans, 1967, 2014), 124.

ACKNOWLEDGMENTS

I have loved thinking about God, writing about His glory, and living with Him through the pages of this book. And He has made my joy more full by calling me to do these things through enriching relationships with people in the body of Christ.

I would like to begin by thanking Don Gates, my literary agent, for representing me in the publishing world. I consider it a gift to have gotten to fly under the wing of a man who knows publishing from the inside out. But more importantly, it has been an honor to work with an agent who has displayed Christ-like characteristics of authenticity, accessibility, and kindness. And though in jeopardy of sounding too simple, it has been fun working with Don—he is an enjoyable person with a great sense of humor!

I also want to communicate my gratitude to Judy Dunagan and the Moody Publishers team for extending an opportunity to partner with them in the gospel. Judy exceeded my expectations of working with a publisher. She displayed kindness by valuing my voice and opinions, while utilizing the gifts and talents of the Moody team to take my work to a higher level of excellence. She also reflected the heart of a Spirit-filled mentor by offering words of encouragement, direction, and specific prayers at just the right time.

I am grateful to my friend Christi Williams, who has a PhD in philosophy from Baylor University, for helping me understand

G. K. Chesterton in *Orthodoxy*. The man is far too brilliant for me to share with others in a thorough way. But I wanted to bring parts of him into this book because he articulates the wonder of God and the adventure of life in a powerful way. It was a joy to get lost and enriched in intuitive thought with Christi alongside the "democracy of the dead."

I am thankful to Don Munton for inviting me to teach this material at Houston's First Baptist Church while writing it. And I am grateful for having gotten to sit under Gregg Matte's kind and humble leadership during this season. I was spiritually born again at Houston's First, and it feels like home to me. Thus, it was a blessing to write this book while in the company of my beloved brothers and sisters in Christ.

I also want to thank my family, friends, Adoring Christ leadership, and prayer team for joining me each week in asking God to produce a book that would exalt Jesus Christ and lead others to experience Him as their all in all. My faith has grown by watching God provide wisdom, inspiration, strength, and spiritual protection through the collective prayers of His people. And I have been refreshed by their friendship along the way.

I am eager to communicate my deep appreciation and adoration for my six-year-old daughter for being willing to share our family love with others. Jade knows I am crazy about her—my family is my first ministry and passion. But through this process I have seen her mind blossom with the beautiful acknowledgment that I also love the bride of Christ—the church. It has been thrilling to see Jade come into the awareness that our family love is expansive—we want to share it with others. And it has been a gift to watch God awaken passions within her to begin serving God's family alongside me.

Most importantly, I want to thank my husband, Bobby, who has loved me and led me throughout the years like Christ. We have traveled together through many joys and hardships in this fallen world on our way to the city of God—even some while writing this book. I am thankful to journey with my best friend and beloved husband, whose faithfulness and strength helps us persevere through the valleys, while celebrating the peaks. Bobby has a Master of Arts in Biblical Counseling from Southern Seminary and is theologically sharp! Therefore, I am also grateful that he has taken time in the midst of the many good works on his plate to read this book and provide profitable feedback throughout. His passion for my purpose and persistent encouragement undergird this work.

Above all, I would like to express my love and gratitude to Jesus Christ, our coming King. It has been the highest honor of my life to know Him and grow toward becoming more like Him. And I still rub my eyes with amazement that He calls us to take gospel adventures with Him. I have fallen in love with Jesus at new levels by considering how His good Kingship will shape the glorious world to come. I have been humbled by His staggering kindness to His bride. I have been inspired to live more fully for Him now. And I can hardly wait to see Him face to face when we stand on eternity's shores—come, Lord Jesus, come! "For from him and through him and to him are all things. To him be glory forever. Amen" (Rom. 11:36).

Bible Studies for Women

N-DEPTH. CHRIST-CENTERED. REAL IMPACT.

AN UNEXPLAINABLE LIFE
978-0-8024-1473-1

**THE UNEXPLAINABLE
CHURCH**
978-0-8024-1742-8

HIS LAST WORDS
978-0-8024-1467-0

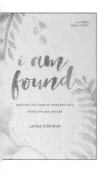

I AM FOUND
•78-0-8024-1468-7

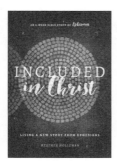

INCLUDED IN CHRIST
978-0-8024-1591-2

THIS I KNOW
978-0-8024-1596-7

**WHO DO YOU SAY
THAT I AM?**
978-0-8024-1550-9

Discipleship Resources

978-0-8024-1382-6

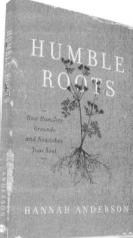

978-0-8024-1459-5

978-0-8024-1340-6

Moody Publishers is committed to providing powerful, biblical, and life-changing discipleship resources for women. Our prayer is that these resources will cause a ripple effect of making disciples who make disciples who make disciples.

Also available as eBooks

MOODY Publishers®

From the Word *to Life*®